ONE STEP
BEYOND
CAUTION

Reflections on
Life and Faith

L. BEVEL JONES, III

LOOKING
GLASS
BOOKS

Published by Looking Glass Books
730 Sycamore Street
Decatur, Georgia   30030
(404) 371-1236

Manufactured in the United States of America
ISBN 1-929619-05-7

To Tuck
Who took a giant step beyond caution in plighting her troth
to me, and has stuck with me every step of the way.

and

In memory of our parents,
Charles E. and Stella Hawkins Jr.
and
L. Bevel and Gertrude Jones Jr.

As life is action and passion, it is required of
man that he should share the passion and
action of his time, at peril of being judged not
to have lived.

—*Oliver Wendell Holmes*

Once to every man and nation,
Comes the moment to decide,
In the strife of truth with falsehood,
For the good or evil side.
Some great cause, God's new Messiah,
Offering each the bloom or blight,
And the choice goes by forever,
'Twixt that darkness and that light.

—*James Russell Lowell*

Contents

Foreword

Many of us need somebody to get us to do what we ought to do. When Tuck and I retired and came back home to Atlanta after our twelve-year sojourn with the good people of the Western North Carolina Conference of the United Methodist Church in 1996, Jerry Eickhoff, Bill Floyd, and Randy Mahaffey chided me for not having written a book. I told them I couldn't sit still long enough to do that, and they said they were going to commission a bright young editor/publisher named Dick Parker, who would sit down long enough and help me put a book together. When I asked what they wanted me to write about, they said my life and ministry. They also asked that I salt and pepper it with a lot of stories.

My life has been a kind of open book. I don't play things close to the vest, but close to the heart. This is not a book of sermons, and it certainly is not a scholarly book. It is very personal—a memoir—intimate reflections on the people, places, events, issues, and ideas that have shaped my life and been the very essence of my vocation. The format is thematic rather than sequential, and the style is conversational. I want you to think of the two of us sitting in front of an open fire and having a heart-to-heart talk.

Bill Gove, master of the art of public speaking, says the secret is self-disclosure. People want to know where you were, what happened, and where you are now. I've done that as candidly and sincerely as I know how in these pages.

The title I owe to the late Dr. Merrimon Cunninggim, dean of the Perkins School of Theology at Southern Methodist University in the 1960s. Addressing a host of us pastors during Ministers Week at Emory as we faced the challenge and controversy of the Civil Rights crisis, he encouraged us to "take one step beyond caution." Step too far ahead and we become ineffective. Stay this side of caution and we never become leaders. One step beyond caution became my stance.

W.H. Auden said he seldom finished a published poem. He finally abandoned it. There is much I would like to have added, and some I probably should have omitted. But here it is. My gratitude to Dick Parker for his guidance, savvy, and patience; to Tuck (Mildred), my dearest friend, closest companion, and wisest counselor; to my children and grandchildren who afford a joy only they can provide, and who have yielded time that should have been theirs in order that "Pop" might pursue what I believe to be "the work of the kingdom"; to the congregations in Georgia and North Carolina who have accompanied us in this pilgrim journey; to my colleagues, who have shared in the pursuit of this High Calling; and to you, dear reader, for giving me a chance to think along the way with you.

A Mother's Faith,
A Son's Faithfulness

"I've done all I can do," the doctor said.

Nothing short of divine power would save the life of the ten-year-old boy lying in a log house in the backwoods of Banks County, Georgia, at the turn of the twentieth century. Penicillin was not yet available to treat the infection that caused the lad's rheumatic fever, nor was there aspirin to relieve his pain. So the doctor closed his bag, walked out of the house, and rode away on his horse. Margaret Jones could only offer her son her continual loving care and her prayers. She knelt beside the bed and gently touched the child's swollen hand. For months the pain had migrated day by day, joint by joint, until his entire skeleton ached, and as he lay curled on the bed, he wanted only to sleep. But the pain would hardly allow it. His labored breathing indicated an enlarged heart, which the doctor feared would soon result in heart failure and final relief. Margaret Jones asked God to spare her son.

Anyone with less faith might have scoffed at the notion. But my grandmother grew up in the holiness tradition, which emphasized the power of prayer and God's active participation in the lives of believers. A number of older ministers later told me they would go out of their way to hear Margaret Harrington Jones pray. She lived daily in the conscious presence of the living Christ and trusted God with childlike simplicity.

After the doctor left that afternoon, she stayed in the room all night with her sick son, praying silently—but ceaselessly. At daybreak she went into the kitchen and prepared breakfast. As the family gathered around the table, she calmly but confidently announced, "Bevel will live." Hence this story!

Healing did not come quickly. The struggle back to health continued for months—over two years in all—and rheumatism remained a thorn in his flesh. I can't imagine my father surviving those two years of invalidism and travail apart from the grace of God.

Dad never dramatized it in conversation or sermon. He refused to be theatrical and manipulate either the gospel or persons. Besides, as a pastor he ministered to scores of people who later died of similar illnesses, or whose loved ones did. He knew you can't standardize faith, make it a cure-all, so that physical survival becomes the litmus test of true prayer and devotion.

What the ordeal and outcome did was to nurture him spiritually and develop in him a deep, steadfast faith. I will share later in this book how I have come to fathom more of the mystery of faith. Suffice it to say at the outset that faith is caught more than taught, coming primarily through experience. I'm having a great time with our sixth grandchild, Jonathan, now two-and-a-half years old. Every day it seems he picks up a new word and is beginning to talk back and forth with us. Faith comes like that. We pick it up in the course of our daily activities, our relationships with others, and the give and take of the community of faith.

Dad was never robust, but he had a robust faith. He inherited absolutely nothing materially, and he never made over $6,000 a year (retiring in 1960). But it didn't bother him. Dr. Gordon Thompson, in his memoir for the Annual Conference annals, said this about him: "Instead of being a restless minister who was always seeking ecclesiastical preferment and professional advancement, L.B. Jones found his highest satisfaction and fulfillment in serving people."

Growing up poor and suffering as he did, Dad developed a faith that enabled him to face every day with the "blessed assurance" that Fanny Crosby—blind from childhood—testifies to in her beloved hymn.

You have noticed, no doubt, that in most kids' drawings a sun is shown shining somewhere—maybe at the bottom of the page. That was Dad. The dominant note of his messages was hope. Not wishful thinking, but devout trusting—confidence in God's abiding presence and unfailing purpose.

There's a story I love about a farm couple in the hills of West Virginia. They were in their latter years in 1938, and one evening the woman was listening to the radio. Suddenly she heard a commotion and turmoil, and thought it was the news. It happened to be Orson Welles' historic presentation of the science fiction drama *War of the Worlds*, in which he imagined earth being invaded by creatures from Mars. She rushed into the next room where her faithful husband was half asleep in a rocking chair. She shook him nervously and said, "John, John, wake up! The good Lord's about to destroy the earth!"

Old John stopped rocking, looked straight at his frantic wife of fifty years, and said calmly, "So what? It's His'n, ain't it?"

At Dad's funeral in 1972 at age eighty-two, Bishop Arthur J. Moore spoke of his "quiet courage." That courage wasn't something he mustered up himself. It was fortitude born of faith. You will find this same strength in the words of Jesus as he walked into the jaws of death at age thirty-three—death by crucifixion. Speaking to His distraught disciples, He said:

> "The hour is coming, indeed it has come, when you
> will be scattered, each one to his home, and you will
> leave me alone. Yet I am not alone, because the Father is
> with me. I have said this to you, so that in me you may

have peace. In the world you face persecution. But take courage; I have conquered the world!" (John 16:32-33)

Bevel lived! Vibrantly, vicariously, victoriously, for eighty-two years. What a legacy:

A good name;

A great purpose;

An indomitable faith.

The Greatest of These Is Love

Lewis Bevel Jones Sr., my grandfather, ran away from home on May 1, 1864, and enlisted in the First Georgia Reserves, Company F of the Confederate Army. He was sixteen years old when Sherman launched his infamous march from Atlanta to the sea that fall. The young soldier came down with the measles and went to the hospital in Macon, Georgia. While there he helped remove minié balls from the bodies of the wounded. He had a propensity for the work, and a doctor said to him, "You can stay and help me and never hear another gun fire."

Instead, Lewis slipped out of the hospital that night and went back to help his outfit resist the west column of raiders until the last battle was fought at West Point, Georgia. He always wanted to be in the thick of things.

Following honorable discharge at Albany, Georgia, on April 13, 1865, L.B. Jones Sr., along with my maternal grandfather, Robert John Carson (also in the Confederate Army) and many other embattled young men, returned to their desolate rural communities to try to get their lives together. Food was scarce, consisting of poke sallet, Irish potato tops, briar leaves, apricot, and pea vines. For vegetables, potatoes and green apples were boiled and mashed together, seasoned with salt, pepper, and onions. When corn was in, roasting ears were often served for breakfast, dinner, and supper.

The clothes situation was just as desperate. A veteran summed it up this way: "One hole in the seat of the breeches indicated captain, two holes a lieutenant, the whole seat out of the pants, a private."

On December 28, 1865, Lewis Bevel Jones Sr. married Margaret Selah Harrison. Starting from scratch, they built a rugged home by the side of the Chattahoochee River in sight of Walker Mountain in northeast Georgia, beating a living out of the red clay fields. Their first child, William Boyd, was born in November 1866, and over the next twenty-seven years Grandma would bear ten more children. (Uncle Willie was married and had a son before my father, the tenth child, was born. Dad would kid about being distantly related to his brother Willie.)

Grandpa was about my size, 145 to 150 pounds, five feet nine inches tall, raw-boned and rugged, and he could ride a horse like a cowboy. Sometime in the 1870s he let his beard grow until it was eighteen inches long—so long that he fastened it under his belt when riding his horse at full speed. He kept the beard for several years until one bone-chilling December day while riding his horse to Gainesville, rain started to fall. By the time he reached town, his beard had frozen stiff. He went straight to a barber shop and had it taken off. His face emerged white as snow. When he arrived home several hours later, his little daughter Emma cried and cried at this stranger who had come into their house.

My grandfather was described as being "as stubborn as a mule and as strong as an ox." When he wanted something he usually got it. He was like the recruit in boot camp near Paducah, Kentucky, where his girlfriend lived. The recruit grew weary and lonely, and decided he would take leave for a day or two. After dark he slipped out and cut through the woods. A security officer stopped him and asked where he was going. The recruit replied, "I have a mother who's dead and in heaven, an old man who's dead and in hell, and a girl who's alive and in Paducah. I'm gonna see one of 'em tonight!"

My paternal grandfather's forebears migrated from Wales to Virginia, then through North Carolina to Georgia. He went to school for less than a year but was determined to become a leader. He bought a dictionary and looked up the words of any printed matter he could find. He turned part of his home into a schoolroom and hired a teacher for his own and the neighbors' children. He and Margaret, his wife, educated themselves and read the Bible from "cover to cover" several times. She taught Sunday school most of her life. Grandpa got to know every authority figure in the vicinity and became influential throughout the county. They took a leading role in developing the Hickory Flat Methodist Church between Lula and Homer in Banks County, and both are buried in the cemetery that Grandpa Jones deeded to the church at the time of his death. My father was licensed to preach from that circuit church that has produced six Methodist ministers.

When he set his mind on something, neither hell nor high water could stop him. Nothing kept him from church on Sunday morning. One January Sunday when the snow piled up too high for wagons, Grandpa wrapped tow sacks around his feet and trudged to church. He arrived back home several hours later, having walked three miles both ways. Grandma asked him how many were there.

"Just me and the Lord," he said.

"What did you do?"

"I built a fire in the potbelly stove, had prayer, and I feel like I've done my duty."

His home was the center of the community with frequent overnight visitors. On Sunday morning he invited any guests to join his family for church. If the guests chose not to come, they'd just have to wait around until the Joneses returned from services.

Grandpa believed his entire family should display his same fierce piety, and he often used a hand or a belt or whatever implement was close by to ensure his children did so. He rarely spared the rod to keep his boys in line.

On one occasion, as he took a belt to his son Sam, he said, "You know what I'm whipping you for, don't you?"

"Yes sir," Sam replied. "For chewing tobacco."

"No," Grandpa said, "I didn't know about that. I'll have to give you another one."

My grandmother had a saintly disposition but was just as firm in her commitment as her husband was. She hated to see her sons abused, although she never scolded Grandpa for punishing the boys. Neither did she sit idly by. Instead, whenever she saw him come at the children physically, she stepped between father and child and took the blow herself. In time, her bruises broke my grandfather's heart and overcame his stubborn pride. He finally fell to his knees and begged forgiveness from her and from God. He said in effect, "If this is what my anger is doing to this dear soul who loves me, I must quit. I must change."

Grandma's love for her children was so great that she suffered with and for them. That vicarious love won their devotion and transformed the spirit of her abusive husband. Love such as that is redemptive.

One evening at a banquet, I entered into a conversation with Chief Justice Hiram Undercoffler of the Georgia Supreme Court. I expressed gratitude for the service he and his colleagues of the judiciary render our commonwealth, and I commented on what he knew so well—that this republic is founded on laws, not human beings.

The chief justice graciously acknowledged my appreciation and quickly returned the compliment, insisting that our work as clergy was even more important because we go deeper, seeking to change human hearts. He elaborated on the limitations of the law and remarked that it is out of the heart that true reform must come.

Six years ago in Charlotte, North Carolina, Dr. Harold Howe hooked me up to a machine that kept my blood circulating, then cut through my sternum and held my heart in his hands. He then bypassed five arteries that were blocked, reactivated my heart, and sewed me back up. Since then I have had a new lease on life.

That's what God wants to do with all of us spiritually. Heed this thirteenth century prayer by Saint Thomas Aquinas:

> Give me, O Lord, a steadfast heart which no unworthy thought can drag downward; an unconquered heart which no tribulation can wear out; an upright heart which no unworthy purpose may tempt aside. Bestow on me, Lord my God, understanding to know thee, diligence to seek thee, wisdom to find thee, and a faithfulness that may finally embrace thee through Jesus Christ, our Lord.

"Bevel-edge, You're Not Going to Quit"

In 1909, at the age of nineteen, with the call of God in his heart and twenty-six dollars in his pocket, L. Bevel Jones Jr. and his younger brother, Sam—who always took up for his less vigorous brother—drove a two-horse wagon for two days over the tiny dirt roads and trails through the mountains to Young Harris, Georgia. They spent the night in the home of strangers who welcomed wayfarers, and found their way to beautiful Brasstown Valley and Young Harris College. Sam went back home, leaving my father in a new world of classrooms and books.

These abject beginnings remind me of another minister of humble origin who said, "Many have gone further in the ministry than I have, but few have come from further back!" Dad used to say that when he arrived at Young Harris he was so green they had to keep the cows away from him. When asked how many grades he had completed, he didn't know, because the one-room schoolhouse he had attended was not divided into classes. So he took a test to determine his capability and learned that he had been educated only to the fifth-grade level. He would have to enroll in the Young Harris Academy rather than the college.

"The toughest part of it," he said, "was being stood down by the eleven-year-olds in a spelling bee."

But Dad lived with that embarrassment and worked his way through the academy and on to the college. He found the religious life at Young Harris reminiscent of life at home. The Reverend Dr. Joseph Astor Sharp was president. With a scholarly mind and pastoral heart, he also served as the local Methodist minister. Attendance at the Sunday night services where he preached was compulsory, as was daily chapel. A biography of Dr. Sharp describes his prayers as "eloquent and sincere, and those Sunday night messages gripped the people who sat before him." The institution was not fanatical in its religious beliefs, but it was intense, and the students knew that it was authentic. It ministered to their deepest needs, and they responded enthusiastically.

Enrollment was small, so Dr. Sharp knew each student personally. He saw my father's determination and potential, and nicknamed him "Bevel-edge." For the six years Dad was there, Dr. Sharp continually nurtured and honed him and became like a father to him. Then in the spring of 1914, still more than a year away from completing his course work, Dad's stomach trouble nearly overwhelmed him. He went to Dr. Sharp and told him he "couldn't take that dormitory food," and would have to leave school to care for his health.

"Bevel-edge," Dr. Sharp said, "you're not going to quit. God's called you to preach, and I'm going to help God fulfill that calling. Mrs. Sharp is a good cook. You'll come take your meals at our house, and we'll get you in fine shape again."

He also excused Dad from classes and encouraged him to go out and chop wood (students worked on the school farm), get plenty of exercise, and enjoy the balmy spring weather. That was great therapy, and in about three weeks Dad was back in good fettle. Dr. Sharp "was not what is called an 'egghead,' " according to his colleague and biographer, Professor Jack Lance (Bert Lance's father). "He knew the common touch. He knew how to deal with people who did not have much education, and he always dealt with them on their own level. This applied not only when he was speaking to them in groups, but when he was talking to them as individuals. He was a great believer in the common people and everything that touched their lives."

A small equestrian statue now stands on the Young Harris campus. Below it is the inscription, "Here the Reverend Artimus Lester, Methodist circuit rider, planted the seed in 1886 that became Young Harris College."

The idea of this man riding through that vast rural circuit of his and seeing the vision of a college on the side of a mountain still stirs my soul. That dream is part of my very being. If you have ever visited Brasstown Valley, you can imagine how excited Artimus Lester was about the possibilities of an institution of higher learning in such a magnificent setting.

For 114 years Young Harris College has inspired similar dreams in the hearts and minds of young people. A Chinese legend advises:

> If your vision is for a year, plant wheat.
> If your vision is for ten years, plant trees.
> If your vision is for a lifetime, plant people.

Years later, after becoming a trustee at Young Harris College, I stopped and focused my eyes on a marble slab on a campus wall that carried the motto of Dad's graduating class of 1915: *Per aspera ad astra*.

I came home and called the reference department of the library for the meaning of those Latin words. The librarian looked it up and read the following: "Through adversity to the stars."

I thanked her, hung up the phone, put my head on the desk, and wept like a baby. I never attended college there, but had it not been for that school, neither Dad's mission in life nor mine could have come about. Before his death we established the L. Bevel Jones Jr. Scholarship Endowment Fund at his alma mater. I can't do enough for that school. To serve on its board of trustees is a deeply satisfying and humbling honor. A similar fund has been established for immigrant students at Young Harris in memory of my only sibling, Kathryn Jones Foster, who died after a valiant six-year bout with cancer at age sixty-seven in April 1999.

Kathryn had a master's degree in social work and spent twenty years as a counselor in the Indianapolis public school system. Upon her husband's death, she returned to Georgia in 1984 and taught English as a second language to immigrant students at Gainesville High School for ten years, guiding numbers of them into institutions of higher learning, including Young Harris.

The Formation of Faith

My father completed his studies at Young Harris College in May 1915, the same month that Germans torpedoed the British ship *Lusitania*. He was obligated to his father, who had reared eleven children and was up in years. Dad could hardly pay him back on a minister's salary, so he returned to Hickory Flat and started selling horses to establish a financial base.

He could not have picked a better time to trade horses, for southern farmers were about to enjoy the greatest prosperity they had ever known. The price of cotton rose from six cents a pound in 1916 to sixteen cents a year later, and continued rising to forty-three cents. Farmers were paying off debts, buying horses, clothes, furniture, and even automobiles.

Dad was a natural salesman, and he loved horses. He could take an old nag and in two or three months groom it, feed it well, get it out in the fresh air, exercise it, and it would be like new. Later, he would do the same kind of thing with people. He was confident he could make a good living selling horses.

The United States declared war on Germany in April 1917, and at age twenty-seven, Dad should have expected to leave home and join the fight. But his bout with rheumatic fever left him unable to touch his right shoulder with his right arm, and he had a bad left knee, the result of a cross-cut saw accident. These disabilities kept him out of military service.

After Dad had been back home selling horses for five years, the Reverend John Yarbrough, presiding elder of the Gainesville District of the North Georgia Methodist Annual Conference, came to Hickory Flat for a meeting. "Bevel," he said, "you're called to preach. You've finished college. Let's line you up for correspondence school at Emory and appoint you to a circuit at Annual Conference this coming November."

Seminary training was not required for pastoral leadership in the Methodist Episcopal Church South. Candler School of Theology, which was the first unit established at Emory University when it was founded in the Druid Hills community of Atlanta in 1914, was still in its formative stages. For ministers like my father who had a license to preach, a college education, and were ready to take a church, Candler offered a complete correspondence course of study leading to ordination and full Conference membership.

Dad anticipated a considerable reduction of income from his days of horse trading, but he had some assets—his car and several IOUs on horses he had sold to cotton farmers in the spring of 1920. Prices were high and cotton markets were eager, so he planned to collect his money when the crops came in that fall, then drive over to Atlanta for Annual Conference in November.

During those good economic times on the farm, Dad had renewed his courtship with his childhood sweetheart, Gertrude Carson, who had grown up on a nearby farm. She was now a teacher who cared for more than her elementary pupils' studies, addressing their more basic needs when their families were unable to do so. For example, she provided toothbrushes and toothpaste to needy youngsters. She most likely took neglected children aside and brushed their teeth for them. Hers was a holistic approach to teaching. She loved her work and loved to help children rise to heights they might never have achieved without her guidance.

Dad wanted to marry Gertrude and begin his career with her at his side. But she was nine years younger than he, and was absorbed in her teaching. In those days she would have been expected to give up her career for the sake of her husband's—to become his helpmate. She turned him down.

Then came an unanticipated postwar economic slump, which sent cotton prices plummeting to thirteen cents a pound. The men who had bought horses from Dad on credit could not pay him back. Suddenly he found himself in financial straits. Still, he had promised the presiding elder he would take a pastoral appointment in November.

Hindered physically and now broke and broken hearted, Dad might have asked God what in the world he had to offer in ministry.

As was true of our Lord after his baptism by John and God's affirmation, "You are my Son, the Beloved; with you I am well pleased," (Luke 3:22), Dad was sorely tempted. He was realizing more and more that we have to find our way by faith, not by sight. Belief, we learn, is not real faith until it is tested. These tests come in various ways and at various times— but come they will, and must.

You are familiar with the famous words of a 1939 Christmas message by King George VI:

> I said to the man who stood at the gate of the year: "Give me a light that I may tread safely into the unknown"; and he replied, "Go into the darkness and put your hand into the hand of God. That shall be to you better than a light and safer than a known way!"

Dad began his pastoral journey by train to Atlanta for his first Annual Conference. The bishop appointed him to follow Dr. Pierce Harris, who had returned to Georgia to preach after playing big league baseball with Ty Cobb and the Detroit Tigers. (Dr. Harris grew to be one of our most dynamic preachers and a public speaker who could charm an audience like nobody's business! Years later he helped me raise money on numerous occasions during my ten-year stint in a new congregation at the beginning of my ministry. I learned much from this master of the pulpit and platform.)

Dr. Harris became pastor of Chickamauga Church, and Dad took the circuit Pierce had served, Kensington, traveling by horse and buggy among four churches in the foothills of Lookout Mountain. There he worked diligently, driven by a love for people and guided by an uncanny intuition that seldom failed him.

A Mother's Prayers
Follow Her Son into Ministry

Although he had left his family and the only woman he would ever truly love, Dad knew he was never alone in his work. His mother made a promise to him before he left Hickory Flat: "Bevel, every week from bedtime on Saturday until sunup Monday morning, I will fast and pray for you and your ministry."

Is it any wonder that my father believed so fervently in the power and practice of prayer?

I suppose one can be a Christian without prayer, but not a very good one. Some years ago I was engaged in a preaching mission for a seminary classmate of mine, Glen Miller, in Greenwood, Mississippi. One afternoon he drove me around the city. As we passed the community hospital, he told me about a recent pastoral visit there with a member of his administrative board.

"We talked for awhile," Glen recalled, "and before leaving I said, 'Let's have a prayer.' He threw his hands up emphatically and said, 'No, no, preacher! I'm just here for tests!' "

In other words, if the tests show serious trouble, come back and we'll pray. But don't you find that you are being tested every day in some way, and stand in need of prayer?

If you experience a bit of guilt when the subject of prayer comes up, you are not alone. It's like our eating habits; we know they need more careful attention. When the apostle says we ought constantly to pray, it is not so much an admonition as an invitation.

When you visit some unique or exotic place, you say to friends, "You ought to go there. Don't miss it!" Even so with prayer. Rather than being ashamed of what we are neglecting, we should be sorry about what we are missing!

The word *religion* means literally "to connect." The deepest longing of our hearts is to connect with the source of our being. Pierre Teilhard de Chardin, the great French paleontologist/philosopher, said, "We are not human beings having a spiritual experience. We are spiritual beings having a human experience." Mark Twain would say that's the difference between lightning and a lightning bug.

Prayer really is doing what comes naturally, although not many of us feel that way about it. Jesus' analogy in John 15 of the vine and the branches is vivid. He is the vine, we are the branches. The branches find their life and sustenance in the vine, which likewise appropriates the elemental resources of sun, rain, and soil. It's the principle of released power.

Prayer takes many forms: petition, supplication, confession, thanksgiving, praise, intercession, and dedication. In essence, it is conversation, not necessarily in words, but in spiritual awareness and communion—a shared presence. Saint Paul talks (Romans 8) about our being children of God. As God's children we are free to call on God as a baby instinctively climbs into the arms of loving parents uttering infantile expressions of need, desire, and trust. The apostle uses the Greek word *abba*, which is the equivalent of the English "da-da," or "daddy."

Paul goes on to admit we do not know how to pray as we ought. That's a master of the art speaking, so take courage. But the Spirit helps us in our weakness by interceding with "sighs too deep for words." Have you not been there? In your distress the words won't come. Your anguish is so acute you don't know how to express it. But you find solace in knowing that God understands and undergirds. I have been there many times, and no doubt will be there again.

Years ago I came across a quotation now lodged permanently in my memory: "God is everywhere, but to find God anywhere, we must meet God somewhere."

I suggest starting with the Psalms. Abraham Lincoln steeped himself in this hymnody of ancient Israel. The Psalms are prayers of petition and praise. You will find virtually every mood, attitude, concern, and desire expressed in them. Let the Psalms prime the pump of your own prayers. When the psalmist speaks of his "enemies," think of all that militates against your well-being: your anxieties, your addictions, your obsessions, your animosities, your habits—anything that holds you hostage and shackles your spirit.

The only way to learn to swim is to get in the water and start paddling and kicking. Likewise, with prayer. We can read all the books on prayer, but we must start praying ourselves and stay with it, realizing that prayer is primarily listening. An old friend, now a centenarian, says his prayers are chiefly two-fold: 1) thanking the Lord; 2) asking God what He wants him to do.

I wish I could claim kinship with the late Dr. E. Stanley Jones, great preacher, spiritual director, and missionary for half a century in India. In his spiritual autobiography, *Song of Ascents*, he tells of a turning point in his faith journey. One morning at his "listening post," lying in bed in an attitude of openness to God, he asked what his agenda should be for the day. He heard the Lord say, "Nothing in particular, but there's something that I want to assure you of: 'You are Mine, and life is yours.' "

From that moment, Dr. Jones said he had his charter of freedom and responsibility. In every circumstance thereafter he found a redeeming factor out of which good came. He experienced increasing fulfillment and lived life joyfully and abundantly. Live with that fundamental reality. It can make a world of difference; yes, even a different world!

Setting Forth from Tobacco Road

After his probationary period in his first pastorate in the northwest Georgia mountains, Dad was appointed by the bishop to a four-church charge in Gracewood, on the south edge of Augusta. While in Kensington he had earned enough to put his old A-Model Ford back into action. This made his 300-mile journey across the state easier than a horse and buggy. He traversed the entire North Georgia Conference, from a northwest outpost to the farthest southeast corner, with everything he owned in that secondhand car.

By the time he crossed into Richmond County, he rolled in on four rims, the narrow tires long since blown. He followed the gully-washed sandy dirt roads across the tops of low ridges and looked out across brown and stunted fields. This was Tobacco Road, where tobacco had long since been replaced by cotton as the crop of choice, and where decades of single-crop cultivation had depleted the soil of any nutrients.

A historical marker along the highway today explains:

> . . . By the 1920s, tobacco was long gone, and so too were the grand estates. Tobacco Road came to hold a less savory reputation as a meandering strip of the poorest, most desolate lands in eastern Georgia. The barren farms scattered along the once-imposing highway were now owned by absentee landlords who had long since left them in neglect.

Erskine Caldwell lived among these very people through the 1920s, and shone a light on them for the world to see in his 1932 novel, *Tobacco Road*. In an introduction to the book, Caldwell described "shabby and dilapidated two-room shacks with sagging joists and roofs," and "hungry people wrapped in rags, going nowhere and coming from nowhere, searching for food and warmth."

Gracewood was a few miles north and east of the most poverty-stricken area, where tenant farmers lived on the very edge of survival.

Caldwell's father was also a minister serving a church near Tobacco Road, and a biography indicates the Reverend Caldwell took a more intellectual approach that was not particularly effective in rural Georgia.

My father's first priority, on the other hand, was to love the people. Although he always wanted to learn more, he was not one to deal with knotty intellectual problems or deep theological issues. Rather, he preached practical, evangelistic sermons and was a devoted pastor.

I kidded Dad one day about the number of books he had written. "Not a one," he said, "but I've rewritten many." He always read with a pen or pencil in his hand and he underlined and scribbled notes in whatever book he was studying.

When he prepared his sermons, he wrote an outline in his big handwriting. He never worked from a manuscript. He read books of sermons by the greatest preachers of his day and would build his sermons with their material, like a bee taking nectar from a flower and making its own honey. He was at his best at a funeral and in prayer. He was deeply spiritual, but never sanctimonious or pietistic. He had a passion for the gospel, and at times God's spirit would flow through him in torrents of inspiration. He had a sparkling personality; people talk to this day about how he loved them and how they loved him—about the confidence and trust they placed in him. I never knew him to mistreat or manipulate anybody.

All of these qualities enabled him to serve effectively among the variety of people who constituted the four congregations of the Gracewood Circuit in the mid-1920s.

And yet, my father knew he could not do the job alone,

even with God's help. His bad leg and arm and his poor digestion continued to bother him. He needed a faithful companion by his side. Those who knew him best sensed a real crisis at that point. He renewed his courtship with Gertrude Carson, and in 1925 she was ready to marry him. She had loved him all along, and had felt guilty for not giving up her teaching and joining his ministry from the start. They were married in June, and together made a terrific team.

Out of that union I was born July 22, 1926, and a week later my father made another commitment that I would not learn about for twenty years. I was in seminary when Dad told me something he had deliberately not mentioned until I had made my own decision to seek ordination.

"Bev," he said, "you know you were born in the parsonage in Gracewood when I served the circuit out there on Tobacco Road. You came two weeks early, (I've been late ever since!), and the doctor couldn't get to the parsonage in time. Mrs. Sego from down the road became an able midwife and brought you into this world. When you were just a week old, I took you into a room alone. Kneeling there, I offered you to God and said, 'Lord, my son is Yours. Use him as You will.' This was a month before you were baptized at Hawkins Camp Ground back home at Hickory Flat."

My sister, Kathryn, was an avid genealogist. She traced our history back to the eleventh century. She even went overseas to pursue it in great detail. She called her work "Jones Bones." She wasn't like the woman who paid $1,000 to have her family tree looked up, then $2,000 to have it hushed up!

Kathryn worked hand in hand with William Bevel Jones, our first cousin who served as the family historian. He was the last grandchild who knew our grandparents and all of our aunts and uncles. He died two years ago, and took with him a wit that rivaled Will Rogers. He passed on much of the historical material in this book.

For some time I played down my rural roots. I did love to visit my country kin, but it was not until time went on and reflection gave me a keener perspective that I came to rejoice in the background and relationships that have shaped my life. Much of it has a mystical aspect, which gives me a sense of mission and destiny.

I am intrigued by Erik Erikson's concept of "ego integrity." This state of being is achieved when we can look back at all that has happened to us—our ancestry and history, the good and the bad—and not only accept, but affirm it. Accordingly, we can look ahead with confidence and trust to make the most of whatever the future may hold. Dag Hammarskjöld, heroic United Nations secretary-general from 1953-1961, summed it up: "For all that has been, thanks. For all that will be, yes!"

Is this not what the sages call the "summum bonum," life's highest good? The Hebrew term is "shalom," a full and complete life. Others call it peace of mind or soul. The poet Robert Browning was shattered when his wife, Elizabeth Barrett, died in his arms in Italy. They were in their middle years. Browning returned to England and accomplished little. He began to study the teachings of the celebrated medieval Spanish rabbi, Ben Ezra. His was a religion of trust, hope, courage, and contentment. Browning experienced renewal and begins his famous poem bearing the rabbi's name with these words:

> Grow old along with me!
> The best is yet to be,
> The last of life, for which the first was made;
> Our times are in His hand,
> Who saith, "A whole I planned;
> Youth shows but half; trust God;
> See all, nor be afraid!

Amen and amen!

The Lost Ball

A garden grows in Athens, Georgia, where a sanctuary once stood. The white clapboard church building at the corner of Chase Street and Boulevard, long since removed, was the place of my first clear memories.

I was three years old when we moved to Athens. Continuing his itinerancy from parish to parish, Dad had been transferred from the Gracewood Circuit to the Crawford Circuit, fifteen miles south of Athens, shortly after I was born. Then in 1929 he was appointed to Young Harris Methodist Church in "The Classic City."

For six years my father stood in the pulpit of Young Harris Methodist Church, and Sunday mornings usually found me sitting on the front right pew with my buddies. Dad let me sit there as long as we behaved. The lessons I learned in that pew, before my tenth birthday, along with the Bible stories my mother told me, formed the foundation upon which I built my faith. Those lessons remain as real for me today as they were over sixty years ago.

The parsonage we lived in stood about sixty feet directly beside the sanctuary, facing Boulevard, which ran downhill for about a hundred yards from Chase Street. One beautiful autumn afternoon I started bouncing a small rubber ball off the front steps. It was brand-new, and Mother, always frugal, had admonished me to be careful and not dare lose it. Eventually a bounce got past me, and the ball rolled down the hill, disappearing into some leaves along the curb.

I began frantically raking the leaves with my bare hands, remembering Mother's stern warning. We were in the heart of the Great Depression. I kept digging and soon became desperate. I couldn't go home without the ball. I wiped my tears and smeared dirt across my face as I gave up hope. Then I heard footsteps, and a familiar voice said, "What in the world are you doing, son, working for the neighbors?!"

It was Daddy.

"You know that rubber ball you and Mother gave me?" I said.

"Sure, son."

"It's gone."

"Gone?"

"I lost it. Mother said, 'Don't you lose that ball,' and I lost it and now I can't go home."

Dad smiled, reached down, took my hand, pulled me up, and said, "Come on, son. Everything will be all right."

As we walked up the hill together, I clung to Daddy like a third leg. When we reached the house, I walked behind him through the front door. Mother came out from the kitchen when she heard the door close. She could tell by my dirty clothes and tear-stained face that I was in distress. Daddy quickly told her what had happened. She rushed forward and clasped me in her arms. That was my first conscious experience of unconditional love. All fear was gone. I could come home even though I had lost the ball.

That simple childhood experience was to become the heart of the message I have proclaimed for over five decades—God's forgiving and redeeming love. It's the greatest story ever told, the best news that ever broke—or ever will.

No soul, no matter the age, is healthy when the chief concern is a half-concealed dread of being discovered—of our true thoughts and deeds coming to light. Peace and assurance come when we know that those closest to us, and particularly the One who knows us best and nonetheless loves us and accepts us. It is the perfect love of God as revealed in Jesus Christ that casts fear out of our hearts. There is absolutely no feeling so secure, so satisfying, as the knowledge that there is nothing we can do to make God stop loving us.

My First, and Last, Smoke Break

The men of Young Harris Memorial Church in Athens had the habit of taking a smoke break between Sunday school and worship service. A buddy of mine was spending Sunday at our house (we were seven years old at the time), and we got the bright idea of following the example of these good laymen by finishing up some of those cigarette butts they so generously left strewn over the church lawn. After dinner we sneaked some matches from the kitchen stove and went into the basement of the church where we began to take a few drags. My conscience was so stricken that it seemed like anybody I heard passing by on the sidewalk above was Daddy.

Presently, sure enough, there came the familiar tread of

his footsteps on the basement stairs. (He had seen us scouring around on the church lawn, and knew we weren't pulling up weeds.) It sounded like the drums of Judgment Day. If we'd had a couple of more minutes and a pair of pickaxes, we could have dug another basement in that church. We hastened to throw the cigarettes away before he appeared, but the evidence was undeniable.

Do you realize what was happening? This was Genesis, chapter 3, all over again. It was the 1933 version of Adam and Eve eating the forbidden fruit. After they had disobeyed God's commandment, they heard the sound of God walking in the garden, and the guilty couple went into hiding among the trees. At least they tried to hide, but it never works.

Brock Amos and I were hiding because we were doing what was forbidden of us and were seeking desperately to get by with it. Again, like the first couple, when found out, we compounded our problem by trying to deny it.

You remember when asked to give an account of their misconduct, Adam passed the buck. "The woman you gave me . . ." You see, he blamed the woman and God at the same time! Then Eve proceeded to make the snake the culprit. Mark Twain wondered how the story would have turned out if they had been forbidden to eat the snake! Twain went on to ask why Adam and Eve should get all the credit for original sin. Said Samuel Clemens, "I could have done it myself." Couldn't we all?

I've been guilty since that incident, and I've seen it so many times in all sorts of human relationships. The seamy side of the bishopric is having to take disciplinary action brought on by clergy misconduct. The transgressions are often made even worse by deceitfulness and dishonesty. I found it to be almost invariable that one who engages in immorality will lie about it. The only way to forgiveness and reconciliation is to be truthful. If Brock and I had acknowledged our misdeed and shown that we were genuinely sorry about what we had done, what followed could have been avoided.

"You boys been smoking?"

"No, sir."

"Let me smell your breath, son."

That did it. Act Two had ended, and the curtain was going up on Act Three in the back bedroom of the parsonage—my buddy being excused, as I suppose a guest should have been. The punishment I got didn't feel good, but do you know what nearly killed me? It was having to face my father. I was so ashamed I couldn't look him in the eye.

This is precisely the reality we often overlook. What makes sin so bad is the alienation it causes. It is not so much that we have broken a rule or a law. We have broken a relationship—betrayed a trust. A woman whose husband had an extramarital affair said to me, "It's not so much what he did with the other woman. It's that he never seemed to care what was happening to me."

Is this not at the heart of the malaise so prevalent in modern society: this inner anxiety, this dis-ease, this insecurity deep within? Oh, we do a pretty good job of covering up, masking it with our frenetic busyness, our urge to splurge, being vogue on the outside and vague on the inside, having more than our share and wondering if this is all there is.

A clergy colleague tells of his annual physical. As he was about to leave the doctor's office with several prescriptions in his hand, the doctor looked at him and said, "By the way, do you have a prescription for this empty, uneasy feeling deep inside of me?"

I learned in the smoking episode and other instances of errancy that had my father not loved me he would not have chastened me. His correction of my actions was an expression of his love.

The God who called Adam and Eve out of hiding is the Father of our Lord Jesus Christ. Assured of this, we can come out of hiding. God seeks us in love and wants nothing so much as to restore us unto Himself that we might be whole again and enjoy that divine fellowship for which we were created.

A Mother's Influence

Modern research has left little doubt that human personality is basically shaped in the preschool years. My sister, Kathryn, wasn't born until I was in kindergarten, so I had the stage to myself and my parents' undivided attention. Mother had given up her elementary school teaching career when she married Dad, so she focused on me all the energy she had previously put forth with a class full of kids. Her name was Gertrude, and "Gert" fit her to a T. Talk about charisma, she exuded it! She could make any game, project, event, or lesson exciting by the way she went about it. We were playmates, and she played with abandon. We loved to make kites and fly them on the big field around Chase Street Grammar School. If you never felt the tug of a kite high in a windy, blue March sky, you missed one of the great thrills of childhood. That was the beginning of my unabated idealism—that upward tug!

One of the first times we flew a kite, I held it and then turned it loose as Mother started running backward with the cord as fast as she could, trying to get it airborne. The kite wobbled its way upward, but didn't go high enough to catch the strong winds. She kept running and tugging that string until she crashed into a good-sized bush, and both she and the kite hit the ground. The sight of her flat on her back frightened me, and I ran to help her. Before I could get there she scrambled to her feet, like a cowboy thrown from a steer, brushed herself off, fumbled around for her glasses, laughed heartily, and shouted, "Let's try it again!"

Mother took every opportunity to create awareness and a sense of wonder in me. This is the heart of true religion, the basic stance of people of faith. It's not gritting your teeth, clenching your fists, mustering up all the willpower you can, and trying to be good. Rather, it is being still and beholding the wonder of creation, and marvelling that anything should be at all, and that you should be a part of it. Reverence and awe are indeed the beginning of wisdom.

Everywhere we went was a kind of adventure fraught with new discoveries. Mother was like Arthur Gordon, who in his book *A Touch of Wonder* tells about his scoutmaster taking the boys on what he called a "silent hike" in the great outdoors. When they finished he asked what they had seen. The Scouts didn't say much. Then after enumerating the many things they had overlooked, their leader exclaimed, "Boys, don't wear your raincoat in the shower."

Nursery rhymes and stories were a nightly ritual. The characters in them became my personal friends, and the moral was invariably driven home. My toys underwent the transformation of Margery Williams' Velveteen Rabbit, and became real by being loved. I can hear Mother now bemoaning the fate of a crippled animal or a fallen sparrow. She would have me virtually in tears over the plight of a neighbor in trouble or some person who was down and out.

But that compassion was coupled with the compulsion to excel. "Anything worth doing is worth doing well," was her watchword. Mother was allergic to mediocrity. Her love was sometimes laced with judgment—a touch of the Pharisee— leading me to toe the line more carefully and to reach a higher level. Thank heaven she never said she didn't love me or wouldn't love me when I fell short or misbehaved. Still, her prodding and challenging were both bane and blessing. She brought out the best in me, but did so at the price of perfectionism.

A Sunday school teacher was exhorting her class of seven-year-olds on personal hygiene. She alluded to John Wesley's famous maxim: "Cleanliness is next to godliness." In concluding her admonition, she wanted to drill it home by reiterating it: "Now remember, cleanliness is next to what?"

After considerable silence, one little girl said, "Impossible."

Ambition is like blood pressure. Without it we can't live. Too much of it, and we die. As I was preparing a microwave meal, I noticed on the package of frozen food, of all places, this sound bit of advice: "Realistic goals lead to a more satisfying, less stressful life for you and your whole family. Certainly do your best, but don't drive yourself toward perfectionism. Instead, cut yourself some slack. Nobody's perfect all the time!" That did me more good than the contents of the package.

Our grandchildren are now where our children used to be, engaging in an endless cycle of activities and engagements. We call it 24/7—twenty-four hours a day, seven days a week. Bishop Mack B. Stokes, my theology professor at Candler, used to say, "The first duty of parents is to survive!"

Worthy parents want the best for their children. Wise parents are careful to discern what the best is. They are also careful how they go about their parenting. One of the mistakes we are most likely to make is to demand too much of our kids, often projecting into them our own failed endeavors and unfulfilled dreams.

The longer I live the more I think about what my folks bequeathed to me and what I am passing on to my children and grandchildren. It is no disgrace not to leave an estate. It is tragic to leave no legacy! What I cherish as an inheritance for my offspring is the wisdom to know what is of true worth and ultimate value. I want them to realize that arrogance and avarice are the origin of sin and the arsenal of evil; that God is love and life is God's gracious gift, to be given back in service to others; that instead of the world owing us a living, we owe the world a life; that one can make a fortune at the cost of an impoverished spirit; that gratitude is the soil in which all other virtues grow and ingratitude is the surest way to break another's heart; that God does not call us to be successful but to be faithful; that the summation of our existence is not in what we have acquired but in what we have become; and most important, that Jesus Christ is the Way, the Truth, and the Life.

The High Calling

From ages six to nine, things really began to happen. My first and only sibling, Kathryn Elizabeth, was born; Santa brought my first bicycle when I was eight; I made my first train trip—alone—a distance of at least forty miles from Athens through Center, Nicholson, and Maysville to Gillsville. Waiting in a two-horse wagon were Uncle Albert and Aunt Pearl Segars, and my cousins Carson and Betty, about my age. We had a delightful two-mile ride to their home, where I spent a week on the farm.

In the fall of 1935, I took my rabbit's foot to Annual Conference in Atlanta and sat with Dad among a host of Methodist ministers to hear the bishop read the pastoral appointments.

In those days there was no consultation, and the clergy didn't know whether they were moving or where they might be going until the bishop read their appointments at the close of the Conference.

I was hoping we would stay in Athens. The clergy were all anxiously waiting to learn if and where they might be transferred. Seeing my rabbit's foot, they asked to borrow it. It passed among them like a collection plate, each one rubbing it vigorously and a few even kissing it. To be sure, that was not good theology, but it was good psychology. It relieved a heap of ministerial misery. Dad was assigned to the Grant Park Methodist Church in Atlanta, and I was in for a major culture shock. It was rougher than a root canal job to leave my friends in fourth grade in the middle of the school year, and at Thanksgiving/Christmas of all times.

Mother and Dad would live in Atlanta the rest of their lives, serving four more churches and moving into their retirement years.

I eventually came to love Atlanta with a passion, but the transition was traumatic. By the following summer the neighborhood kids were beginning to accept me, and I was gaining confidence. A trip to Washington with the Schoolboy Patrol was a real growth experience, and the move to Hoke Smith Junior High School was a milestone indeed!

In social studies we were asked to write a paper on some vocation, and mine was on the ministry. A minister was all I had ever thought of being. On Mother's Day 1939, I was in my customary seat on the front row at the evening worship service. Our neighbors' son, Bobby Dorsey, was next to me, along with half-a-dozen other young people. Dad waxed eloquent in a sermon about the premier prophet, Elijah, who passed his mantle on to Elisha, thereby anointing his young protégé as his successor. The thought that had been incubating in my brain and heart came alive that night. I experienced a summons to follow in my father's footsteps, to become a leader like Dad in the life and work of God's people. When Dad called for any who wanted to dedicate their lives to God, I shifted sleeping Bobby Dorsey over to the shoulder of the next person and stepped forward, kneeling at the altar. I do not remember what Dad said or I said. That kind of tryst is by nature indescribable. It was a moment of truth. My life's purpose, my reason for being, came into focus.

I had no idea what all of that entailed, but I knew what I was to be and do. I have never regretted or questioned it. Instead, I have been steadily fulfilled.

Oh, I've had my days, indeed my "dark nights of the soul." Dr. Fred Craddock, master of the art of preaching, says that he is glad to be dedicated to a cause that does not depend on how he feels about it on a given day.

Ordained ministry is more than proclamation, but as someone has observed, preaching is to the gospel what the point is to a spear. It became for me a consuming passion. That's one reason I had qualms about the possibility of the bishopric. Years later, I often reminded my people that I was elected a bishop, but I was called to preach. My own bishop, Joel McDavid, reassured me, however, that the episcopacy affords a superb vantage point for proclaiming the Word. I later found in twelve years of appointing ministers that at the top of the "want" list of the churches was a pastor who could really preach. In the church renewalist period of the 1960s and '70s, preaching—and even corporate worship—was deemphasized. I hung tough for vital worship and strong preaching along with social action. Both preaching and corporate worship have come back with a flourish. I wonder, though, if sometimes our preaching doesn't come across like professional wrestling—more exhibition than real competition. Harry Emerson Fosdick described preaching as struggling with individuals over questions of life and death, and drenching a congregation with your own life's blood.

Since I was a youngster of nineteen, mine has been the high privilege and magnificent obsession of being a "steward of the mysteries of God," and a herald of God's amazing grace. I can say with Isaac Watts,

> I'll praise my Maker while I've breath
> And when my voice is lost in death,
> Praise shall employ my nobler powers.
> My days of praise shall ne'er be past,
> While life and thought and being last
> Or immortality endures.

My First Steps Beyond Caution

My first performance before an audience was a triumphant experience. Shortly before Christmas 1931, two of my five-year-old friends and I, wearing bathrobes and turbans our mothers had wrapped around our heads, walked slowly toward the manger singing with trembly soprano voices, "We Three Kings of Orient Are." The experience made an indelible impression on my young mind, and the wise men themselves could hardly have felt so important as we.

The performance, however, was out of character for me and only possible because of my fellow sojourners. I was, in fact, painfully shy, and would battle timidity continually.

Age elevated me to a more prominent role in the annual

Christmas pageant a couple of years later. I was to recite Luke 2. This time, however, with the spotlight on me alone, I froze. Mother and I had rehearsed for days, and I knew it by heart. I mumbled the first words of the opening sentence, "And it came to pass . . ." then I went blank.

Sitting on the front row, Mother whispered anxiously, "that a decree went out from Caesar Augustus . . ." But the words would not come. Abjectly I bowed my head, let the tears roll, rushed to her side, and curled up under her arm.

My career in public speaking was off to an inglorious start. In fact, right then I never wanted to stand before an audience again.

When we moved to Atlanta from Athens the following year, I experienced more trauma. We were three months into the school year, and the Thanksgiving/Christmas season was upon us. I knew no world other than the small town of Athens, and now I was suddenly thrust into a big city full of strangers.

I walked into Jerome Jones Grammar School, and the very first day I heard boys whispering about that new "preacher's kid." I cringed because preacher's kids were immediately suspect.

My parents spelled my name "Beve," and some of my schoolmates pronounced it "Beevee." That did nothing for my self-esteem either! Fourth graders love to tease and even taunt.

I toughed it out, believing that this hazing would be temporary, and I determined that I would somehow prove myself to my peers. You may know the story of the boy whose doting mother drove him to school each morning, walked him to the door, hugged and kissed him and reluctantly said goodbye. Then she rushed back in the afternoon, met him at the door, hugged and kissed him and breathlessly asked, "And what did Mama's little darling learn today?"

One day he came out with his clothes dirty and torn, one eye black, and his nose bleeding. His mother hugged him fervently and cried, "What did Mama's little darling learn today?"

Back came the retort, "I learned another boy not to call me 'Mama's little darling.' "

I soon came to love sports, and athletics helped me gain confidence and build friendships. I joined in with the kids on the street to skate or in the park in the afternoons to play ball, or in the yard to shoot marbles. I was relatively small and often the last to be chosen for a team, but I was dead set on being part of the action. Two of the bigger boys would choose sides. Sometimes after everyone else had been selected, one of them would look over at me and say, "You can have Jones." That hurt, but being part of the action was what really mattered.

When baseball season started in 1936, I discovered one of the great joys of living in the city. Tuesdays and Thursdays were Boys Day at Ponce de Leon Park, home of the Atlanta Crackers minor league baseball team. We boys got in free. We didn't mind the two-mile walk, and we sat along the right field line in a special section reserved for kids. We banged the empty seats when we wanted a pitching change or our team to rally.

Every summer I spent a couple of weeks in the country with relatives, and observed nature in the raw. The quickest way to learn the facts of life is on a farm. My new city friends, however, were no dummies, and quite explicit in explaining to me the difference between boys and girls, where babies came from, and who Santa Claus really was. I was so naive that until we moved to Atlanta, I still believed in the Easter bunny! As my innocence vanished and I became streetwise, I was fully accepted as a member of the "'hood." You might call it the extracurricular education of young Bev Jones. It comes sooner or later, for better or worse, for everyone.

Halloween was far from trick or treat in those days. It was all trick in the Grant Park community, but nothing violent. Weapons were virtually nonexistent. The older kids in the community didn't hesitate to soap store windows and street-car tracks so the trolley couldn't make it up the hill, and pester neighbors. One night several of them managed to perch a "Baby Austin" automobile, a bit smaller than a modern Volkswagen, on the porch of a house. I was too small and timid to do that kind of thing. I just stood back a safe distance and took delight in their mischief.

I began to learn that I would have to step out if I was going to amount to anything. I wanted to see all the baseball games I could, and make some money too, so I pushed against my bashfulness and walked up to the vendors' quarters at Ponce de Leon ballpark on the first day of the season. I stood there with fifteen or twenty guys ranging from my age (eleven) to over sixty, all hoping to be chosen. As usual, I held back a bit, but hung in there and was hired to sell peanuts and Cracker Jacks.

At first my inclination was to walk quietly along the aisle holding my peanuts, waiting for someone to call me. I soon learned from watching the other guys that you have to assert yourself if you're going to sell anything. I began to holler and did fairly well. I earned a promotion the next year to selling Cokes, and was on my way, seeing the game and making money at the same time!

The next step was to Grant Field and Georgia Tech football. I got a job selling Cokes in the East Stands. This was where the out-of-town folks sat, and the warm afternoon autumn sun bore down really helping business.

One Saturday afternoon near the end of my eight-year stint as a vendor, Tech was playing Notre Dame. The weather was unusually warm, and the Cokes were going great. In the second half a man sitting spraddle-legged at the top of the aisle right along the 35-yard line steadied himself with one hand and beckoned to me with the other. He was obviously inebriated and feeling no pain.

"Fellow," he called out as I approached, "come on up here a minute. I want that whole case of Cokes. I'm going to set everybody up on this row," he said reaching out with his right hand. Then pointing in the other direction, he added, "And everybody on that row.

"I've got the money," he added as he pulled a roll of bills

that looked like a head of lettuce. That convinced me, so we emptied that case. I told 'em, "They're on the house!" Then I brought a new case and we sent them the other way.

When we had served everybody in both directions, the man laid a ten-dollar bill, two fives and several ones on the step and said, "Here you are, buddy?"

I restrained myself and kept only the ten spot. Forty Cokes at twenty cents left me with a two dollar tip. Everybody seemed happy, especially the donor. I didn't feel too bad myself!

That was more than fifty years ago, and ever since that Saturday afternoon I've been trying to cultivate in people the spiritual equivalent of what that man had. He threw caution to the wind in his desire to make others feel good, and in his strange way, he succeeded.

Saint Paul said, "God loves a cheerful giver" (2 Corinthians 9:7).

"Audacious" is the literal meaning. Try it.

I heard about a young pastor whose crowd was smaller than usual one sabbath because of the weather. He called for the offering, and when the ushers returned to the altar with it there was hardly enough money to cover the bottom of the plates. He lifted the plates and his face heavenward and said, "O Lord, as you can see, there aren't many of us out today, and those who are out aren't out very much!"

Many conscientious Christians have resolved the whole matter with the master plan: *tithing*. I was taught it, have continually practiced it, and heartily recommend it. It's a wonderful spiritual regimen, helping to keep priorities in proper order. My favorite passage of scripture along these lines is Paul's second letter to the Corinthians. The apostle is taking up a collection in all the faith communities he established around the Mediterranean to strengthen the home church in Jerusalem. He cites as a shining example of audacious giving the saints in Macedonia. Despite a severe ordeal of affliction, their abundant joy and their extreme poverty had overflowed in a wealth of generosity. They gladly gave according to their means, and even beyond their means, "begging earnestly for the privilege of sharing in this ministry." (II Corinthians 8:1-5)

When have you heard of people *begging* for the privilege of giving? But read further for the secret: "They gave themselves first to the Lord, and by the will of God, to us. . . ."

The golden text of the Bible, John 3:16, states "God so loved the world that he gave . . ." God is love, and love expresses itself in giving. It's that simple. We may give without loving; we cannot love without giving. Kahlil Gibran, in his classic *The Prophet*, catches the spirit of it:

> There are those who give little of the much which they have, and they give it for recognition and their hidden desire makes their gifts unwholesome.
>
> And there are those who have little and give it all.
>
> These are the believers in life and the bounty of life, and their coffer is never empty.
>
> There are those who give with joy, and that joy is their reward.
>
> And there are those who give with pain, and that

pain is their baptism.

And there are those who give and know not pain in giving, nor do they seek joy, nor give with mindfulness of virtue;

They give as in yonder valley the myrtle breathes its fragrance into space.

Through the hands of such as these God speaks, and from behind their eyes He smiles upon the earth.

A New Perspective

One of the most exciting experiences of my childhood was our class visit to the state Capitol. I was fascinated by the statues and huge portraits. But the truly breathtaking part came when we climbed the stairs and stepped out onto the platform surrounding the dome. We all thought for sure we could spot our neighborhood in the distance. That was the highest I had ever been, and the world was a lot larger than I imagined. My horizons were widening.

The following spring brought the biggest event of my young life. I was a schoolboy patrolman at Jerome Jones Grammar School, wearing a badge and sash and helping my classmates cross the street before and after school. In 1938 a throng of patrol boys rode trains to Washington, D.C., where we stayed for four days. We had a huge parade down Pennsylvania Avenue to the U.S. Capitol one day, all of us from Atlanta wearing white short pants, blue shirts, and navy caps. The policemen traveling with us took us under their wings and let us experience the aura that is unique to the citadel of the free world.

On our third afternoon in Washington, my group was to visit the Washington Monument. Mother had told me that I had to take at least one bath while I was there. I took my towel and my place at the end of the line outside the bathroom down the hall. When my turn finally came, I hurried in and out of the dirty tub, dried off, and ran back down the hall, which seemed strangely quiet. I dressed as fast as I could and raced down to the lobby. It was empty except for a friendly policeman. I was stunned. Sensing my plight, the officer came over, put his hand on my shoulder sympathetically, and said, "Son, I'm sorry, but they've all gone to the monument." Then looking at me from head to toe, he added, "But you sure are neat and clean."

Though bitterly disappointed at not going to the top of that towering monument, I saw enough to titillate my eager mind with the grandeur of our nation's capital. What we had studied about in history class came alive and helped instill in me a deep love for my native land and gratitude for so rich a heritage.

As I have grown I have come to the realization that true

patriotism is not "America—love it or leave it." It is "America—love it and improve it." Democracy is everybody's business, and it is always under construction. The danger is not that it will be destroyed from the outside, but that it will suffer by default and corruption from the inside. Remember the fellow who, when asked what he thought about the threat of ignorance and apathy in society, shrugged and said, "I don't know, and I don't care."

I always looked to the late Norman Cousins for insight and perspective. In his classic *Human Options*, Cousins observed that democracy's main problem is people who take themselves lightly historically. Too many of us have no real awareness of the myriad bricks that had to be put in place one by one over the centuries for us to live in the penthouse of freedom. He went on to name among the benign enemies of free society clergy who by word and deed foster the feeling in their congregations that the chief purpose of churches and synagogues is to provide social respectability for their members; clergy who dispense balm but do not quicken conscience. There's merit in the old saying that preachers are supposed to "comfort the afflicted and afflict the comfortable."

I can't remember when religion has been more prevalent and popular than right now. Everybody is talking about faith and spirituality. That's fine, provided it is the real thing. And what is the real thing? Jesus summed it up in one great commandment: "You shall love the Lord your God with all your heart, mind, soul, and strength, and your neighbor as yourself." That's a mighty tall order!

In the model prayer, Jesus begins with the familiar term, "Our Father." God is intimate. But that salutation goes on to affirm, "Who art in heaven, hallowed be thy name." That same intimate deity is also infinite and holy—to be revered and obeyed.

In 1986, I was asked to offer the opening prayer at the Democratic National Convention in Atlanta. I spent more time on that brief invocation than on many sermons. I made it non-partisan. (Dr. Bernard Fitzgerald tells of a young preacher who had just moved into a new parish. This was back in the late 1930s. In his pastoral prayer one Sunday he said, "Lord, bless President Roosevelt." Then remembering that he was in an overwhelmingly Republican community, he quickly added, "and Lord, I mean Teddy, not Franklin.")

I prayed for our country and our world. Then I stressed the thought that I had worked hardest on, and which was the burden of the prayer: "God, we do not ask that you bless what we do, but that we may do what you *can* bless." God by nature is altogether righteous. Therefore God cannot tolerate, let alone bless, that which is not upright. Dr. M. Scott Peck has written a book with the arresting title *A World Waiting to Be Born*. It is a call for civility, and his thesis is "consciously motivated organizational behavior that is ethical in submission to a Higher Power." Isn't that what Lincoln had in mind when he added the phrase "under God" in his Gettysburg Address, and what we mean when we recite the same words in our pledge of allegiance to the flag of our own country?

A poignant story tells of a woman engaged in her daily devotional. She prayed earnestly for a better world, writing a list of the things she would do to help bring it about. Then she signed her name to it and symbolically offered it up to God, only to hear the response, "No, thank you. Take another sheet of blank paper, sign your name at the bottom of the page, and I will fill it in."

Faith in Search of Understanding

Senator Zell Miller was born and reared in Young Harris, Georgia, and became a professor at Young Harris College. His father was a professor before him, and his name is on my father's diploma. Senator Miller tells about the installation of chimes years ago in the belfry of Sharp Memorial Church on the campus. One day an old-timer was passing by the church while the chimes were sounding forth. The young boy who was assigned to operate the chimes asked the old fellow how he liked them. The passerby cupped his hand around his ear and asked him to repeat it. Finally he said. "Son, I'm sorry, but I can't understand a word you're saying because of them damn bells!"

Faith did not come easily for me after I graduated from

high school. I grew up in a simple, sheltered environment. I guess you could call it intellectual innocence, but I soon discovered there is no virtue in that! I had a naive, greenhouse faith, and I was determined to protect it.

When I went to college I soon found myself overwhelmed. I was like the proverbial blind man in a dark room looking for a black cat that wasn't there. Or to change the metaphor, I was so deep inside a tunnel, I could not see light at either end. I took the account of creation in Genesis literally—though there are two different stories—and now in college I was discovering that the earth is millions upon millions of years old, and that humans had evolved from lower animals. I had my beliefs about God and Jesus and the Bible wrapped up in a neat little package, and now I was faced with an onslaught of contradictions and questions that literally tore me out of my frame of reference.

I went to see my philosophy professor, Dr. Leroy Loemker, and told him that I was committed to the ministry, but I was afraid I wouldn't have much left to preach, the way we were going. This was two weeks into Philosophy 101. He was too wise to offer me quick reassurance. "We've just begun, Jones," he said. "Why don't you stick with me?"

I did, for five more courses in philosophy. Dr. Loemker turned me every way but loose. The only way out of the tunnel was through. There was no backing up. I began to see that just as I had shed my baby teeth to make way for my permanent teeth, I was going to have to shed some of my juvenile ideas. Ole Josh Billings had something when he observed, "It is better to know nothing than to know what ain't so."

I began to doubt, and found that doubt is not a sin. Honest doubt is the doorway to further understanding. Suppose Copernicus had never questioned Ptolemaic astronomy, which said the earth was the center of the solar system? Suppose English barons had never challenged the divine right of kings to absolute rule, and had not presented King John with the Magna Charta in the meadows of Runnymede on July 15, 1215?

What if the Apostle Paul had not risen above his pharisaical tradition and opened his mind to the new truth that was in Jesus? Even after his conversion, Paul kept searching, realizing that we see through "a glass darkly," or "a mirror dimly." "We know in part," he acknowledged and spoke often of the mysteries of God. I have come to terms with the reality of mystery and the mystery of reality. In moments of exasperation, Tuck will look at me in dismay and allow that I am still a mystery to her! Nothing new about that. She is often a mystery to me, and I to myself! I'm akin to the old Quaker, who said somberly to his wife of fifty years, "Methinks everybody is a bit peculiar, except thee and me, and sometimes I have my doubts about thee."

I have my doubts about those who have no doubts. The pure and simple truth is seldom pure and never simple. Recall the famous dictum of Justice Oliver Wendell Holmes, who insisted that he wouldn't give a fig for simplicity this side of complexity, but he would give anything for simplicity on the far side of complexity. I can get simplistic answers to my physical ailments at the barber shop. What I go by, however, is the simple explanation my physician gives me after the complexity of his medical training and all the research in which he engages. Some of us never solve our problems because we answer them too quickly.

There is a prayer from Kenya in our United Methodist Hymnal:

> From the cowardice that dares not face new truth,
> From the laziness that is contented with half-truth,
> From the arrogance that thinks it knows all truth,
> Good Lord, deliver me. Amen.

Do you not find Christ's promise that the Holy Spirit will guide us into all truth (John 16:12) reassuring as we face the bewildering issues of the twenty-first century? God didn't stop speaking when the Bible went to press!

My friend and colleague Dr. David McKenna offers sound advice as we seek to live out our faith: If you can't think it, don't believe it; if you can't sing it, don't preach it; if you can't live it, don't push it."

I once thought higher learning was a threat to my faith. On the contrary, it informed and strengthened my faith. I took my creed out of the greenhouse and exposed it to the nurturing elements of earth, sky, and sea. Like Saint Augustine, I found that "where I have sought truth, there I have found my God, the truth itself."

I can honestly say that as I have preached and practiced the gospel for over half a century, it is self-authenticating. I now have fewer articles in my creed, but more faith in God. I remember well hearing the great theologian Albert Outlar in one of his last lectures admonish us amid all the perplexities of our time, "Hold fast to Christ, and for all the rest—hang loose!" Christ is the one fixed point in the kaleidoscope of human experience. He is indeed the "Life, the Truth, the Way."

Since a youth I have cherished John Oxenham's poem, "Credo" (italics mine):

> Not what, but *Whom* I do believe,
> That in my darkest hour of need,
> To mortal man can give;
> Not what, but *Whom.*
> For Christ is more than all the creeds,
> And his full life of gentle deeds
> Shall all the creeds outlive.
> Not what I believe, but *Whom.*
> Who walks beside me in the gloom?
> Who shares the burden wearisome?
> Who all the dim way doth illume,
> And bid me look beyond the tomb
> The larger life to live?
> Not what I believe,
> But *Whom.*
> Not what,
> But *Whom.*

Black and White in 1947

While a seminary student, I worked for the YMCA in what was called its Gra-Y program. I was a football coach for sixth-grade boys at Highlands Grammar School in Druid Hills. We practiced on Tuesdays and played other teams on Fridays. In the fall of 1947 I gathered a group of twelve-year-old boys at Springdale Park on Ponce de Leon Avenue near Briarcliff to begin the football season.

Sitting on the bank was a black boy the same age as the others. Several of them knew him and asked if Thomas could join us. I wasn't about to say no. I was especially glad when I saw how good an athlete he was. He looked like another Jackie Robinson in the making. Robinson that very year had broken

66

the color line in Major League baseball, taking the Brooklyn Dodgers to another level, but enduring insults and epithets wherever "dem Bums" played.

Our first game was at another school. I called Moss Causey, head of the Gra-Y program, for his guidance. Since this was without precedent, we agreed I would have to use my own judgment and see what developed. I knew all the other coaches, and it would be no problem for them. As for the parents, we would have to play it by ear. None of them raised a concern throughout the season. They did comment on the way Thomas ran around, over, and through their boys. But he was a perfect gentleman in doing so.

By November the season was going better than I had anticipated. The boys were proud of Thomas, and made him part of the team in the fullest sense. I wished the whole city could have seen how these youngsters—separated by institutions, customs, laws, and in almost every aspect of their lives—got along together.

The last game of the season was against Mary Lynn School, across the street from Candler Park. At halftime our two teams were gathered under trees about fifty yards apart. A city employee who had been watching us intently while cutting the grass on his tractor stopped some distance away and motioned for me. I sensed what was going to happen, and wanted to avoid an incident if at all possible. He spat on the ground near his feet and said, "What's that nigger doing in the park?"

I drew up my back and said, "You mean that colored boy?"

He repeated the nasty word, and then said, "You know it's a city ordinance, and niggers are not supposed to be in Candler Park."

I tried to reason with the man, but he threatened to call the police. My anger turned to remorse when I saw my players standing and looking my way. I walked slowly to them, dreading to have to tell them what must happen. I went over and tapped Thomas on the shoulder and asked him to step aside. The words didn't come easily. They were about as difficult as any I have ever uttered. A lump formed in my throat as I told him that because this was a city park and his skin was not the color of ours, he could no longer play. He was not even supposed to be in the park. I let him know how upset I was about it, but that we had best obey the law and not cause more trouble.

Of course, I told him how proud I was of him, what an outstanding athlete he was, and what a fine man I knew he would grow up to be. He didn't say a word, just lowered his head and ambled away. Few experiences in my life have been as heart rending. What we had violated that autumn afternoon was far more than a city ordinance. We had violated the dignity of a child of God.

The whole team was saddened and subdued. They had seen the city worker, and I think they knew. I told them what I had told Thomas, and said I hoped that someday they, along with me, could help make things different. The coach and the boys on the other team kept discretely quiet. They knew what was happening too.

We lost that day—not only the game, but a lot more. It was an awful ending to a wonderful season. Nonetheless, a seed had been planted in the hearts of the boys on our team, the idea that as human beings our similarities are much greater than our differences. We've been learning gradually and painfully over the half century since that we must live and work together as a team, all of us, whatever our race, color, creed, or cultural background.

G.K. Chesterton put it graphically: "We are all together in the same boat on a stormy sea, and we owe each other a terrible loyalty."

We took a chance, ran a risk to nurture that idea and allow it to grow—for a few months at least—in the fall of 1947.

Hearing God's Call in the Cuban Hinterlands

My first real step beyond provincialism was to Cuba in 1948. I was a middler in theology school, and the Methodist Church's Cuba Caravan, which sent theology students and undergraduates on evangelical missions, was just getting underway. Two of my classmates had gone as pioneers the previous two summers, and they coaxed me into it. I had studied Spanish in high school and college and was fairly conversant in it. My companions were Nancy Black, a junior at Wesleyan College; Megdalia Abreu, and Mimi Fernandez, college students in Cuba; and Miss Nize Fernandez, a teacher at our Methodist school in Matanzas, our Caravan mother.

We traveled across the island together, spending a week in

each of nine different churches. We adapted to the culture, customs, and circumstances of these rural and urban congregations, with activities for young and old from early morning until about 9 P.M. daily. In those pre-Castro days, the government did not interfere with the work of the churches. But under the dictatorship of Fulgencio Batista, the people were stifled. Ownership of land and resources by large corporations from outside the country did not foster self-development of the Cuban people.

The Methodist Church had been in mission there for decades. Candler College in Havana (1912), named for the same leader as Candler School of Theology, Bishop Warren Aiken Candler, was a vital force. Dr. and Mrs. Maurice Dailey, missionaries from the States, were invaluable in helping with our orientation and supporting us throughout our stay. I could write a book about that summer, but I want to mention two persons who impacted my life profoundly.

The first is Razziel Vazquez, a young bachelor pastor in Aguada de Pasajeros. This is an out-of-the-way, tiny town on the eastern edge of the swampy, thickly wooded Zapata Peninsula. Razziel was a mulatto, a prepossessing, handsome, dapper young man who was groomed as if he had stepped out of a bandbox. He lived in the church, or maybe it's more accurate to say the church was in his house—a small house at that! It was more like those churches described in the book of Acts than anything I had seen in the United States.

Razziel greeted me enthusiastically as my host for the week

71

and showed me the modest bed I would sleep in and the closet for my clothes. (My colleagues stayed in other homes.) The closet contained a number of fine suits he had bought when he was a successful tradesman. I knew immediately that this individual had experienced a dramatic Christian conversion. Nothing short of that would have caused him to sacrifice such a prosperous career to serve in a place like this. Razziel showed me the privy out back, a "room with a path." The only water came from the rooftops into cisterns. We took our meals on a flimsy table covered with brown paper. Neighbors prepared food and brought it to us—layered meals of beans and meat and rice in tin pails. I wondered who had mixed it and how clean it was, but was careful not to offend anybody. I recalled the words of a former missionary: "I've eaten a lot of dirt for Christ's sake."

These good people were sharing out of their overwhelming poverty with a generosity that bordered on divine. When bedtime came, Razziel showed me how to drape the one mosquito net that he had over my bed. The windows always remained open, and there were no screens. He did without a net for the entire week. That was the kind of love I would see expressed by the Cuban people throughout our journey.

Razziel and I awoke early the next morning and quickly prepared for church. By 6:30, eight people had gathered in the house for a prayer meeting and Holy Communion. The population of Aguada de Pasajeros was a mix of fair-skinned Hispanics, descendants of former African slaves, and island natives.

My host led the service, and I assisted him. As I prayed I said, "Perdonos los pescados," which means, "Pardon our sins." Or so I thought. But after I said it, I felt the altar rail shaking as the worshipers tried to control their laughter. I knew I had made a blunder. Razziel told me later that I had said, "Pardon our fish." The word for sins is pecados. (But I know some people who need pardon for the fish stories they tell!)

After our communion service, Razziel and I went out into the street, where he preached with a gusto reserved for tent revivals back home. His message was emphatically evangelistic. His impact on that village was tremendous!

Again, I took my turn at it and tried to get to know the local people, asking one elderly woman informally, "¿Esta en estados?" which I thought meant, "Have you been to the States?" She smiled and blushed and modestly said no. As we walked away, caravan mother Nize began laughing and said, "You asked her if she was pregnant."

I made my linguistic mistakes with enthusiasm, giving the folk a lot of fun. Our errors in the language actually drew us closer because they knew we were trying. Isn't it strange that wherever we Americans go abroad we expect everybody to speak English? Nor do we tip our flag like every other nation does in the ceremonial parade opening the Olympic Games.

In our few days together Razziel and I became such good friends we agreed that I would come back to visit him someday, and he would visit me in the United States. Tuck and I visited him and his new wife, Isuada, in 1951. They now live in the Miami area.

The next person to make an impact on me was Onell Soto. His circumstances were even more meager than Razziel's. Onell lived in *el campo*, in other words, out in the country some distance from Omaja, another out-of-the-way village that looked like a deserted mining town in the Old West during the days of the California gold rush. Omaja lay in the hinterlands near the Sierra Madre Mountains of eastern Cuba, where Fidel Castro was stealthily building up his revolutionary forces. About the only transportation was a train that ran through the town early in the morning and late in the afternoon. It was the biggest event on any given day!

I stayed in a home with no running water and no electricity. Animals joined us at and around the table. I usually got to the house after my host family had gone to sleep, and stumbled my way to bed with a flashlight. Miss Sara Fernandez, from Tampa, was the beloved missionary who led the activities of the community in a white frame church. The population of greater Omaja may have numbered up to 500. At least 100 gathered each day for activities. Onell, age fifteen, rode his bicycle in from the backwoods. He was usually the first to arrive and the last to leave. He had been brought up in a Christian home and was one of those vibrant, charming youngsters who grabs your heartstrings at first sight. A born leader, he was eager to be about the work of the Lord.

Onell spoke little English—he pronounced my name

"Dreft" (like the detergent)—but a mixture of both languages enabled us to establish rapport. We bonded during that week, and I told him of my confidence that God had great things in store for him.

I observed my twenty-first birthday that week. Megdalia, Mimi, Nize, Onell, and a few others celebrated it with a fried chicken dinner at Sara's parsonage. That dear bird was poorer than Job's turkey! But it was a beautiful gesture nonetheless.

Onell graduated from the University of Havana in 1956, then came to the United States following Castro's rise to power. He accepted God's call to preach and a few years later was granted a scholarship to attend the University of the South in Tennessee. He became a priest in the Episcopal Church, and eventually was sent to Venezuela where he became a bishop.

When Tuck and I retired and returned to Atlanta in 1996, Onell was serving as assistant bishop of the Episcopal Diocese of Atlanta with offices in Saint Philip's Cathedral. It was a thrill being together again with this outstanding leader of the church and getting to know his fine family. He is now bishop in Birmingham, Alabama. What a classic story of how God works wonders with people of obscure origin, meager resources, and a burning vision!

To Love and to Cherish

They say a picture is worth a thousand words, but when a picture is all you have, it can mean all the world to you. During my ten-week visit to Cuba, I sometimes became homesick, so I opened my wallet and gazed at a picture I had cut out of the *Emory Wheel*, the student newspaper. The young lady in the picture had been chosen by John Robert Powers as queen of the college yearbook in 1948. She was a student at Wesleyan College in Macon. Emory was all male in those days, so the queen came from another school. Mildred Hawkins was her name, but the Wesleyan girls called her "Tuck," for Kentucky, her home at the time.

Tuck and I first met the previous summer at Camp Glisson,

our Methodist Youth Assembly at Cane Creek Falls in the mountains near Dahlonega, Georgia. Through the years Camp Glisson has played a unique role in the life of our family. Tuck and I were active there as youths, and our children and grandchildren have in their times relished youth camp. We bought a cabin at Glisson in 1964 that remains to this day a "haven of blessing." We spent many a Friday night and Saturday there during the years when we were a parsonage family, and still find it a place of rest and renewal.

Thousands of young people have had religious experiences and developed friendships at Glisson that have impacted their lives immeasurably. The camp is seventy-five years old and in a process of renovation, with enrollment at a peak. Tuck and I are deeply moved that the leaders of Camp Glisson have proposed a family renewal center to be named in our honor.

In early fall after my return from Cuba, my caravan sister, Nancy Black, invited me to lead vespers at Wesleyan College in Macon, where she and I would talk about our experiences in Cuba. To be honest, the hidden agenda was to get Tuck and me together. I asked Nancy to make sure Tuck was there and free afterward, but not to tell her what I planned. Tuck remembers Nancy telling her as she dressed for vespers that day, "Don't you think you ought to wear something nicer?"

I don't remember what Tuck wore to vespers, but I do remember that she was as pretty as the picture I had looked at so many times. My mind was not altogether on my presentation at vespers since Tuck was in the audience, and I did get her to go with me to a local drive-in restaurant for a snack following the service. Thus began a dating pattern that took me to Macon or brought her to Atlanta every weekend until we were wed nine months later.

The Reverend Harvey Holland Sr. had asked Bishop Moore to appoint me as his associate at Decatur First Methodist Church. It was my last year at Candler, and Tuck was in her senior year. Curfew at Wesleyan was at midnight on Saturday, and I got her back to the dorm not a minute before. The drive home was over two hours, and I had to be at the church the next morning in time for the first of two worship services, beginning at 8:30.

Brother Holland's sermons were sound and substantive, but he was not a dynamic preacher. By the middle of the same message at the second service, I sometimes struggled to stay awake in my chair by the pulpit. When friends kidded me about my head nodding, I assured them that I was simply agreeing with everything Bother Harvey was saying.

After a few weeks at Decatur I received my first good tip in the ministry from Miss Sarah Flake, secretary to Dean H.B. Trimble of the Candler School of Theology. She was a member at Decatur First, and the kind of person who could set you straight and not make you mad. She took me aside one day at school and said, "Bev, for heaven's sake, get rid of those white ribbed socks. With your dark blue suit and legs crossed in that pulpit chair, they look like neon lights in a cemetery."

Tuck's father was pastor of First Methodist Church in Ashland, Kentucky, and she invited me to visit with her and her parents over Christmas break. Before leaving I shopped for just the right Christmas gift, and finally settled on a nice string of pearls—not precious, but expensive for me. Then I made the full-day trip by car to Ashland, which is on the Ohio River. When I reached town at dark, I went to the YMCA to get cleaned up before following the directions to the Hawkins' parsonage home. It was actually attached to the sanctuary on a main midtown thoroughfare.

I pulled up to the curb at about 7 P.M., grabbed that beautifully wrapped box of pearls, laid it on the front fender, got my baggage from the back, closed and locked the doors, paused to check my image in the window, and took one more lick at my thinning hair. I wanted to look like Beau Brummel for that all-important appearance. I skedaddled up to the front door, nervous as I could be, and rang the bell. Tuck appeared, more gorgeous than ever. Right behind her stood her parents, handsome and hospitable: the Reverend Charles E. Hawkins of Franklin, Tennessee, and his wife, the former Stella Harris, of Decatur. Tuck introduced us graciously, and they welcomed me into their home, ushering me upstairs to the room in which I would stay. Just as we got to the top of the steps, it hit me like a bolt of lightning: THE PEARLS! I had left them on the fender on that busy city street.

Tuck says she doesn't remember my saying a word, not even "Excuse me." I ran down the stairway like a scalded dog, and out the front door in a flash. Almost as beautiful as Tuck was the sight of that box of pearls unmolested on the fender of that 1941 Plymouth.

Meekly I strolled back to the house, where Tuck and her parents stood in amazement. I stammered out an explanation of my panic. We had a good laugh at my expense, and I succeeded in making a lasting impression—for good or ill—on my future in-laws.

Five months later, on Mother's Day 1949, I called Brother Hawkins and politely asked for his daughter's hand in marriage. I kidded him about her knowing what she was getting into, being a PK and growing up in a parsonage. He responded favorably, and then good-naturedly said, "But I must warn you; she can't boil water."

I thought he was joking, but found out three months later he was telling the truth—like a man of the cloth should.

Dr. Lester Rumble, my first district superintendent, was a classmate of Brother Hawkins at Candler School of Theology and had been in his wedding to Stella Harris in the chapel at Decatur First Methodist Church in 1922. He and Brother Holland did the honors in our wedding on August 12, 1949 in that same sanctuary. My best man was the Reverend Wesley Stephens, whom I had known since age three in Athens. A year later I stood beside him as he pledged his faith to Annette Akins. Wesley insists to this day that he was the best man in both of our weddings. He goes on to add, "Bev is a man of his word. He kept telling Tuck when they were courting that he wasn't good enough for her, and he's been proving it ever since."

Tuck knows me better than I know myself, but loves me

anyway. Her devotion has been without reservation, and so has mine for her. We've come to know what Antoine de Saint Exeuprey meant when he said that mature love is "two persons looking together in the same direction." Faithfully we have shared our lives and this ministry. She has borne with me patiently as we have itinerated from place to place and moved into ever more extensive fields of service and mission. Not only has she been unselfish regarding my hectic agenda, but she has let me unload my burdens into her forbearing heart. She has believed in me in my times of self-doubt. She has honored the marital vow, remembering always that the question is not, "Are you in love?" but, "Will you love?"

The Reality of Tragedy

The summer of 1949 could hardly have been more eventful. Tuck graduated from Wesleyan College, I from Candler School of Theology; we got married, and I became the founding pastor at the first new Methodist congregation in Atlanta after World War II. Dr. Lester Rumble, superintendent of the Atlanta West District, had conducted a survey and found fifty people who agreed to join the new church in the Audubon Forest subdivision of Cascade Heights in southwest Atlanta. On Sunday, July 3, Dr. Rumble introduced me to the people at the Adams Park Library, our temporary quarters, and the next Sunday I was on my own.

The excitement of those first few months was indescribable, as our fledgling faith community began to take shape. It grew like kudzu. We closed the charter in early September with more than 100 members, and by the end of the decade received 1,950 persons into our fellowship. I knew them all personally—where they lived, what they did for a living, the names of their children, and in some cases their pets! We became a family of God.

Tragedy struck early. A six-year-old girl was run over and killed on the sidewalk in front of her home by a drunken driver. Then came the death of a two-year-old boy overnight in his bed. After that, Captain Doug Volk, a dynamic leader in our congregation who had three boys, ages three, five, and seven, was the first Delta pilot on a regular commercial flight to crash and die as a result of wind shear near the airport in Shreveport, Louisiana.

That sort of thing has been duplicated many times in my half century of ministry. I have had my share of tragedy in my own family, and no doubt you have experienced similar misfortune. We cannot help but wonder why there is so much suffering in the world. The question has tantalized the minds of sages and saints through the centuries.

Popular opinion runs the gamut from simplism on one extreme to cynicism on the other. Many take refuge in the belief that it is simply "God's will." Others identify with Archibald McLeish, who in the introduction to his play *J.B.*, writes: "If God is God, He is not good. If God is good, He is not God. Take the even, take the odd."

We must admit that there is no purely rational answer to the horrible happenings that raise questions about either God's goodness or God's power. There's a story about a professor of religion who was discussing the problem of evil with a class of sophomores. He was pointing up its unfathomable nature when he noticed one student fast asleep. Suddenly the teacher called his name and asked, "Do you have an answer to the problem?"

Not wanting to prove that he had been asleep, the student abruptly replied, "I'm sorry, sir. I did know, but I've forgotten."

With sharp satire the professor exclaimed, "My young friends, mark this day well. In the span of recorded history only two persons have known the answer to the problem of evil: Jesus, the Son of God, who did not tell us, and our fellow student—and alas, he has forgotten!"

While there is no patent explanation for why bad things happen, there are mitigating factors.

• God has given us freedom to think, choose, and act on our own. As a result, we sometimes hurt ourselves and others with our poor judgment.

• God has put us in an unfinished world, giving us the privilege of participating in His ongoing creation. For example, houses are still trees until we cut the lumber. The thrill is in the adventure of building and developing, but so is the risk of accidents.

• God has established the universe on natural laws, and set in motion physiological phenomena that make life possible, but also make it precarious. Tornadoes, floods, and other disasters occur as a result of a vast network of cosmic forces.

The term "act of God" should be used very carefully. Dr. Leslie Weatherhead, great British preacher of another generation, wrote a classic seventy-five-page book entitled *The Will of God*. It came out of the travail he experienced with his congregation during World War II and the Nazi blitz of London. Weatherhead sees God's will in three dimensions:

> God's intentional will
> God's circumstantial will
> God's ultimate will

God intends our good, our well-being. God is the father of our Lord Jesus Christ. When we say something is God's will, we must ask the question, "Would Jesus do such a thing?"

God doesn't intend all that happens to us, but he *superintends* it. The circumstances may be such that God has to allow the consequences, such as a person being injured or killed in war. War is certainly not what God intends for human beings, but given the circumstance of war, all sorts of catastrophes occur. While everything doesn't come from God's hand, it comes *through* God's hand. That is to say, God has a hand in it. God is ultimately in command and will, through His providential grace, fulfill His benevolent will in and through us.

The supreme illustration of this, of course, is the crucifixion and resurrection of Jesus. God took the most heinous form of punishment in the first century and made of it the very means of our salvation. Through Jesus' death, God defeated death, giving us confidence not only in life eternal, but of the final triumph of truth, goodness, and love.

Tuck's father served the Tennessee and Kentucky conferences of the Methodist Church for thirty-five years before his untimely death at age sixty. It was said of him that he was not partial toward anyone. Rather, he was partial to everyone. He loved and cared for his flock with deep devotion. Scribbled in his own hand in his funeral manual are the words of Helen Keller: "The world is full of suffering, and the overcoming of suffering." This is the very heart of scripture. Holy Writ does not try to explain the problem of evil. It offers something better—the capacity to overcome it. Instead of being cynical because of suffering, we can make of it a sacrament, a means of God's grace. We can become stronger in our faith. My own belief in this is validated by observing countless gallant souls, who in a losing battle against illness and adversity became "more than conquerors," achieving the victory that overcomes the world, even our faith.

One of the preachers whose writings nurtured me was Dr. Joseph Sizoo. I have drawn solace continually from his story of a professor in New Testament who came in his course to the book of Romans and that magnificent eighth chapter in which the Apostle talks about suffering and asserts that "in everything God works for good for those who love him, who are called according to his purpose." (8:28 RSV)

A student raised his hand and asked pointedly, "Professor, do you believe that?" The professor responded, "I believe it with all my heart."

That afternoon the professor and his wife had an automobile accident. She was killed and he was mortally wounded. The university president rushed to the hospital, stood at the bedside of his dying colleague, expressed his sympathy, and asked, "Is there anything I can do for you?"

"Yes, Mr. President, there is. Please go to my New Testament class tomorrow morning and tell them that what I said this morning about Romans 8:28 still holds true."

They buried the professor and his wife side by side, and on the tombstone were inscribed the words, "In all things God works for good with those who love him and are called according to His purpose."

A New World View

In the fall of 1956, Dr. Frank Morehead, Dr. Rembert Sisson, and I were invited by Bishop Arthur J. Moore to accompany him on a world tour. We worshiped one Sunday in the American Church in Paris, France. As soon as I heard the organ strains of "My Country 'Tis of Thee," a lump came in my throat. Then when we began to sing, tears welled up in my eyes.

The bishop had been asked to come to India as president of the General Board of Missions to participate in the centennial celebration of Methodism in that country. Bishop Moore loved to tell about being turned down as a missionary by the Board of Missions when he was a young minister because of his lack of formal education. He was made bishop at age forty-one and became president of the Board of Missions. He traveled abroad more than 100 times. He would kid about not getting to go first class when he applied for missionary service, so he ended up going second class as a bishop!

Since India was halfway around the world, our trip was planned to circle the globe, with stops all along the way at Methodist points of interest. My Audubon Forest congregation graciously allowed me the time off, and even paid my way. Dr. Paul Worley, then at Candler School of Theology as director of development, held forth as interim preacher.

London: Wesley's Empassioned Message for Us

This global venture confirmed both my love of America and my world citizenship. It reinforced my Methodist heritage and at the same time heightened my appreciation of other faiths.

Our first stop was London, where we saw firsthand the scars of World War II and of Hitler's blitzkrieg. We stood awed in Saint Paul's Cathedral, which survived while buildings all around it were severely damaged if not destroyed. A London minister told us of an awful night when bombs created an inferno. "Amidst the flames and fury of the blitz, I saw the majestic dome of Saint Paul's Cathedral, still standing in all its splendor. I was reminded then that righteousness is supreme. God will prevail. We cannot give up."

That British minister's words echoed the sentiment of

Bishop Moore's oft-stated dictum, "Nobody can believe in the sovereignty of God and the saviorhood of Christ and not believe in the ultimate supremacy of righteousness."

My fascination with John Wesley, which began in seminary, was heightened by seeing where he actually lived, labored, and preached. I marveled at this fastidious man, who said "cleanliness is next to godliness" then traveled more than 200,000 miles on horseback. He went to the factories and mines, reaching out to the masses.

He sent Francis Asbury as his emissary to Colonial America in 1771, and later ordained Thomas Coke to join Asbury and his gallant circuit riders in formally constituting the Methodist Church as a denomination in 1784. Wesley himself never returned to this country, but continued his arduous labors in England until his death in 1791 at age eighty-eight.

Some say that Wesley's ministry of personal evangelism and social righteousness saved England from the equivalent of the French Revolution. He was ahead of his time in the ecumenical dimension of ministry, seeing the world as his parish. His global vision helps us understand how we can be loyal to our native land and devoted to a particular brand of Christianity, and still be brothers and sisters to people of other countries, denominations, and faiths. God's love transcends all these human categories, classifications, systems, and institutions.

A favorite clergy story is about two men of the cloth who differed strongly in their theological views. They almost came to blows one day in an argument over doctrine. Finally they simmered down and realized that their behavior was unbecoming of the clergy. One patted the other on the shoulder and said, "Let's stop this fussing and go about our Lord's work together—you in your way and I in *His* way."

It may well be that future historians will see the movement of people of faith across the earth toward unity as the most significant phenomenon of the twentieth century.

Uppermost in our prayers should be the prayer of Jesus as recorded in the seventeenth chapter of the Gospel According to John. It is called the High Priestly Prayer of our Lord as He interceded for us and prayed earnestly that we would be *one*. God calls us to unity amid diversity, affirming our similarities instead of accentuating our differences.

The tragic irony of God's people through the centuries is that Christianity itself often becomes a bone of contention rather than a tie that binds. We tend to make Jesus the very source of our divisiveness, quarreling over exactly who our Lord is, what the church should and should not do, and what precisely it means to be a Christian. My colleague Dr. George Wirth of First Presbyterian Church in Atlanta shares an illustration of how tedious and tacky the strife among us has been at times. He tells of the "lifter controversy" back in 1783, which split the church of Scotland right down the middle over how the chalice of wine should be lifted above the communion table. One group said the raising of the cup was a liturgical act that emulated the Roman Catholics. The opposition declared that it wasn't so. After two years of heated debate, these

Presbyterians decided to go their separate ways. Wirth goes on to quote Dr. Frederick Buechner in his book *Whistling in the Dark*: "When Jesus took the bread and said, 'This is My body which is broken for you,' it's hard to believe that even in His wildest dreams He saw the . . . brokenness of the church as His body."

I can hear Jesus saying to religious leaders today what he said to Simon Peter at breakfast on the shore of the Sea of Galilee after His resurrection. These were his last words to the one who was to become the head of the early church: "Simon, do you love me?" (John 21:15) Notice our Lord did not ask Peter what he believed about Him. He asked whether he loved Him, and He asked repeatedly. Notice further that Jesus would not take yes for an answer. He wanted action, obedience, faithful ministry: "Feed my sheep; tend my sheep." That defining moment in the life of the first leader of the Christian church is still the watchword for God's people today. The authenticity of our faith is found not so much in doctrine as in devotion and discipleship.

Rome: The View from the Vatican

Jerusalem and Rome are key to any understanding of our history and appreciation of our heritage as a people of faith. A visit to the catacombs brought home to us dramatically the courage of the ancient monks who meticulously preserved priceless manuscripts, perpetuating the biblical faith once delivered to the saints. The remains of the Coliseum virtually cry out against the barbarism of the ruthless imperial leaders and extol the virtues of the heroic Christians who were literally fed to the lions. Lions are no longer involved, but the persecution is taking place with horrific fierceness and frequency in the modern world. We see it and read about it day after day: Cambodia, Bosnia, Ethiopia, Oklahoma City. Crimes of hate. Humanity is ever exhibiting both the noblest and the grossest behavior of all God's creation—and that choice goes on forever.

Of course, we visited the Vatican, where six years later Pope John XXIII would convene Vatican Council II. The pontiff exhorted all the Catholic faithful to take an active and intelligent part in the work of ecumenism—reaching out to non-Catholics in good faith. This momentous council led to a sea-change in Protestant/Catholic relations. In the early days of my ministry, we Protestants celebrated Reformation Day in October with a litany of things that distinguished us from the Roman Catholic Church. Today we stress what we share in common and our mutual mission. Echoing from the epochal Vatican Council II are the papal words, "Let them cooperate especially for the sake of Christ, their common Lord: let His Name be the bond that unites them!"

Two of my dearest friendships over the last twenty years are with Archbishop John Donaghue, of the Catholic Archdiocese of Atlanta, and Bishop William Curlin, of the Catholic Diocese of Charlotte. The archbishop and I were together for a decade in Charlotte. He was then made head of the Atlanta archdiocese, and upon my return to Atlanta he and I have lunch now periodically and work together in the Christian Council of Metropolitan Atlanta. Bishop Curlin succeeded Archbishop Donaghue in Charlotte and extended great care to me during my open-heart surgery in 1995.

It was he who brought Mother Teresa to Charlotte, where several of us met with Mother Teresa privately before she spoke to an awed crowd in the Charlotte Coliseum. We accompanied her to the stage, and when she finished her message, she came around and greeted each of us and spontaneously handed me her manuscript. You can be sure it has a hallowed place in my archives. This wonderful soul has been an inspiration through the years. Two things about her ministry are especially significant to me. She said repeatedly, "If you are looking for Jesus, you will find Him most surely in the faces of the poor." Then, "Ministering to the sick and dying is our opportunity to do something beautiful for God." A priest who was among a group who had been to Calcutta to visit with this "Sister of mercy" says he asked her what one message she would send to her colleagues in the United States. She replied, "Tell them to pray, 'That I will not get in God's way.' "

One of the high moments for me in the Charlotte area was receiving the Cuthbert E. Allen Award from the Ecumenical Institute of Wake Forest University and Belmont Abbey College.

How important it is for us to realize that while being grounded in our own faith we can be hospitable and cooperative with people of other faiths. There is profound wisdom in the time-honored maxim of the ecumenical movement:

> In essentials, unity.
> In nonessentials, liberty.
> In all things, charity.

Jerusalem: The Unholy Holy Land

Oddly enough, Bishop Arthur Moore, who traveled overseas a hundred times, never visited the Holy Land. Even on our world tour, he had to branch off on a side trip to the African continent because of a crucial conference in Elisabethville, Belgian Congo. The others of us traveled on to Beirut, Lebanon, then one of the most beautiful cities on earth. From there we went across "no man's land," a heavily guarded narrow strip of land separating East and West Jerusalem. This was only eight years after the partitioning of Jerusalem to establish a homeland for the Jews following the ravages of the Holocaust, and only eleven years before the 1967 Arab-Israeli war. The perennial conflict between Jews and Arabs goes back to the days of Abraham. After only a few days in Jerusalem and seeing thousands of Arab refugees huddled in flimsy hovels against the mountains of Jericho, I knew that it was going to be exceedingly difficult to work through the partitioning of the land and the resettlement of displaced Palestinians.

There are no simple answers. Suffice it to say that even as Jesus wept over Jerusalem, surely our Lord weeps over the plight of Jerusalem and the Near East today. We must never cease to "pray for the peace of Jerusalem," and work for justice and security for all concerned.

Another eye-opening experience for me in the Near East was the sight of Bedouins carrying transistor radios and listening to European and American news and music. They were learning about people the world over who stirred their imaginations and aroused their ambitions. I saw firsthand technology bringing the world together and could see the emerging "revolution of rising expectations," among the down and out of the earth. Dr. J. Wallace Hamilton aptly described this phenomenon as the "Thunder of Bare Feet."

I saw it in Pakistan and in India as we continued our travels. People who had known only despotism or colonialization were beginning to claim their full human rights. They were laying the foundation of a worldwide struggle for liberation, following the example of our own American Revolution.

Let us not forget that the Bible has a bias for the down and out, the marginalized, the disinherited, the oppressed. It begins with the liberation under Moses of a people in Egyptian bondage. Our Lord was born to peasant parents in an out-of-the-way province ruled by a Roman governor under the imperial authority of Caesar Augustus. Jesus began His public ministry by making His platform unmistakably clear: "The Spirit of the Lord is upon me, because he has anointed me to bring good news to the poor. He has sent me to proclaim release to the captives and recovery of sight to the blind, to let the oppressed go free, to proclaim the year of the Lord's favor" (Luke 4:18-19).

I was greatly encouraged in the summer of 1974 when I had the opportunity to participate with Dr. Billy Graham and a host of clergy from across the globe at a conference in Lausanne, Switzerland, on "world evangelization." It was at this conference that the more conservative branches of Protestantism openly affirmed the social dimensions of the gospel. Dr. Peter Storey, great South African Methodist preacher and leader in the overthrow of apartheid, calls it "prophetic evangelism," and defines justice as "love distributed." In addition to changing people's hearts and minds, it also seeks to change systems and institutions that lack integrity and fail to offer equal opportunity to all.

This reality was brought home to me vividly in the narthex of the cathedral of Belmont Abbey near Charlotte, North Carolina. A baptismal font is mounted on a big rock. The inscription reads: "From this stone, on which persons once were sold into slavery, they now are baptized into freedom."

A Defining Moment

The politician was asked what side of the issue he was on. After a bit of deliberation he replied, "Some of my friends are for it. Some of my friends are against it. As for me, I'm for my friends."

There come times when each of us must decide whether to risk whatever we have attained and take a stand that is unpopular but morally imperative. When I review my half century in the ministry, I derive more satisfaction from a step I took in 1957 than just about anything else in my professional life.

The stirrings around the country in the mid-1950s were unmistakable after the Supreme Court decision in May 1954 declaring that schools separated by race were inherently un-equal. Black citizens were tired of second-class treatment and were prepared to stand up for their rights. Unrest pervaded white neighborhoods, and fear laid hold of many in my neck of the woods.

We were developing a brand new congregation in the fron-tier subdivision of Audubon Forest. New houses were going up overnight. Some of the occupants were moving out from West End, where increasing numbers of African-Americans were establishing residence around Atlanta University, the larg-est aggregation of black students in the United States. People generally were anxious to settle down after the turmoil of World War II. Governor Herman Talmadge's defiance of the Supreme Court's action as "cheap politics" and his pledge of "perma-nent segregation of the races" was music to many ears.

I was fresh out of seminary and just married. People were flocking to the churches. The temptation was not to rock the boat. Keep everybody happy. Don't deal with anything con-troversial.

Dynamic social/political/ethical forces were converging. My conscience would not let me stay this side of caution. In 1954, the Reverend Razziel Vazquez traveled to the United States from his tiny Cuban hometown of Aguada de Pasajeros. The Reverends Wesley Stephens and Lewis Davis and I, who had worked with Razziel in Cuba, wanted him to experience our country and be our guests.

Razziel rode a bus from Miami to Atlanta. Because of his

race, he had to ride in the back of the bus and could not eat in the same restaurants as other passengers. He was weary and crestfallen when he arrived. I knew my own race-sensitive congregation would hardly welcome him. I didn't want to force the issue, so I took the path of least resistance. Knowing the Emory University community to be more open and cosmopolitan, I contacted my friend Dr. Candler Budd, pastor of Glenn Memorial Methodist Church on the campus, and told him of the situation. He said he would be glad to have Razziel worship with him and his congregation.

That move hurt Razziel, I am sure, but it hurt me more. My shame caused me to redouble my efforts in leading people to the realization that as Christians we could no longer perpetuate a segregated church and society. My passion was to help free us all from the shackles of prejudice and to grow in the grace of Christ.

I saw two extremes preparing for a confrontation that would affect us all. My thinking began to crystallize around the philosopher Hegel's dialectic—bringing the thesis and the antithesis together in a viable and valid synthesis. One extreme held that white and colored should be separated, period. The other extreme insisted that we must do away with all forms of segregation immediately, no matter the cost.

Here the advice of a colleague proved to be wise counsel: "Not dead center, but the dynamic middle." He was talking about resolving conflict with integrity. We need to keep in mind, however, that the dialectic won't work unless there are persons bold enough to represent the antithesis—the avant-garde position.

The situation heated up even more in 1957, when African-American children in Little Rock, Arkansas, attempted to attend an all-white school. Arkansas Governor Orval Forbus challenged the federal government, and President Eisenhower sent troops to Little Rock to enforce desegregation. That, of course, intensified concern across the entire South. Many politicians advocated closing the schools rather than to allow integration. As a minister, I knew I must use whatever influence I had to help keep that from happening.

Then Dr. Roy O. McClain, influential pastor at First Baptist Church, Atlanta, said, "Pulpits have been paralyzed . . . the well-informed people have been quiet." *The Atlanta Journal and Constitution* reported his statement, then invited clergy to express themselves on the issue through the columns of the newspaper. Dr. McClain led the series of articles by writing, in part:

> Those who refuse to speak often fail to remember that freedom is placed in jeopardy more by those who refuse to exercise it than by those who will not permit it. Our security is not in being mute. There are times when silence is golden, and there are times when silence is yellow.
>
> The past three years have fanned the flames of racial hatred to white heat. The seed of bitterness will germinate for decades to come.

His statement echoed my sentiments, and I knew I had to do more than talk to my congregation about the matter. I was ready to risk "going public." I talked with Dr. Harrison McMains, who was then executive director of the Christian Council of Atlanta, and he brought together a group of about a dozen of us who had taken Dr. McClain's cue. We met privately at Columbia Theological Seminary in an effort to make a concerted response, and come up with some basic convictions about the current crisis. We asked Dr. McDowell Richards, president at Columbia, to serve as our "Thomas Jefferson" and draft a statement we would present to the public. We gathered and reflected on his first draft, suggested changes, and he developed the document further. We met again and modified it slightly and agreed to go with this:

> These are days of tremendous political and social tension throughout our entire world, but particularly in our nation and beloved Southland. Because the questions which confront us are in so many respects moral and spiritual as well as political, it is appropriate and necessary that men who occupy places of responsibility in the churches should not be silent concerning their convictions. . . .
>
> In presenting our views for the consideration of others we can speak only in a spirit of deep humility and penitence for our own failures. We cannot claim that

the problem of racial relationships has been solved even in the churches which we serve, and we are conscious that our own example in the matter of brotherhood and neighborliness has been all too imperfect. We do not pretend to know all the answers.

We are of one mind, however, in believing that Christian people have an especial responsibility for the solution of our racial problems and that if, as Christians, we sincerely seek to understand and apply the teachings of our Lord and Master, we shall assuredly find the answer.

Then we listed six principles which we held to be of basic importance:

• Truth is mighty and will prevail.

• As Americans and as Christians we have an obligation to obey the law. . . .We have no right to defy the constituted authority of the government of our nation.

• The public school system must not be destroyed.

• Hatred and scorn for those of another race, or for those who hold a position different from our own, can never be justified.

• Communications between responsible leaders of the races must be maintained.

• Our difficulties cannot be solved in our own strength or in human wisdom. . . . It is necessary that we pray earnestly and consistently that God will give us wisdom to understand

His will; that He will grant us the courage and faith to follow the guidance of His Spirit.

This is a moderate, even mild statement, today in the first years of the twenty-first century. Nearly fifty years ago, however, it was a blockbuster.

Almost as important as the document itself was our method for gathering support for it. We decided not to mail it, for our adversaries could get hold of it and sabotage our efforts. Instead, the clergy comprising our core group glued the manifesto to tables at several designated churches. Then we wrote a letter to all Atlanta area ministers whose addresses we could obtain, asking them to go by and read our manifesto, and if they would support it, to sign their names. Eighty of the hundreds of local clergy put their signatures on the dotted line.

With the support of those eighty, we took the manifesto to Ralph McGill, editor of *The Atlanta Constitution*. McGill had been using his column to champion the rights of blacks for years, and we had informed him privately of what we were doing. He gave us the front page, publishing the entire manifesto and the names of those who had signed it under the page one headline, "Racial Beliefs Cited by 80 Pastors Here."

It was Sunday morning, November 3, 1957, and I didn't know what to expect at our young Audubon Forest church on the corner of Sewell and Willis Mill Roads in southwest Atlanta. Many of our parishioners had moved out of West End to avoid living among black people. I had recruited most of them personally, and served among them for eight years. They knew of my concern about race relations. I had spoken out often on the issue, always speaking the truth in love. Many of them disagreed with my stance, but respected me nonetheless.

I received a number of cold stares that morning as the congregation gathered. Several members asked some serious questions, although no one was antagonistic. The general public reacted more aggressively. My phone rang often in subsequent days, and I received letters so hot I needed asbestos files. A few of them reflected adversely on my ancestry.

In time our efforts began to have a salutary effect, not only in Atlanta, but across the country as the news spread. We even heard from missionaries and leaders abroad. My congregation was understanding, if not supportive, of me in my work with the Christian Council of Metropolitan Atlanta. More ministers around the city began to assert themselves. In 1958 we updated the manifesto and 315 ministers signed it.

When Prayer Becomes Real

My fellow seminarians and I laughed when our homiletics professor, Dr. G. Ray Jordan, told us, "There may come a time that you will think the Holy Spirit has left you, when the truth is, your liver isn't functioning well."

We thought he was joking. Then in 1960 I came to understand what he had meant. I indeed wondered whether the Holy Spirit had forsaken me.

After a decade as pastor of Audubon Forest Methodist Church, Bishop Arthur J. Moore appointed me in 1959 to First Methodist Church in LaGrange, Georgia, a college town. Dr. Waights G. Henry Jr., president of LaGrange College, also invited me to teach a course on church administration to pre-ministerial students. Besides that, the congregation at First Methodist had committed themselves to build a new sanctuary. I began writing a weekly article for the *LaGrange Daily News,* and was in the early stages of what I have called the flip side of my ministry—inspirational, motivational speaking with humor. This has put me in touch with a host of people I would never have reached from the pulpit, and has resulted in friendships that continue to enrich my life. Like Pogo, I was surrounded by insurmountable opportunities.

A typical overachiever, I have trouble setting limits. After preaching the memorial service at Annual Conference in June 1961, I returned to LaGrange, cut the grass on Saturday afternoon, and went to bed that night worn to a frazzle. Sunday morning I awoke so tired and achy I could hardly get up and go to church. I feared the worst because hepatitis was reported across the country, and numerous people around LaGrange had come down with it. Dr. William B. Fackler had told me earlier that I was showing some signs of it.

Preaching the sermon that day was like crawling uphill backwards, and I felt energy draining from me as I forced my way through the message. When I finished the sermon, I got Tuck's attention and asked her to have Dr. Fackler come to my study as quickly as possible. Bill took one look at me and knew right away I had hepatitis.

"What can we do about it?" I asked.

"Not much of anything," he said. "Bed rest is essential, along with nourishing food. There's no medication for it. You simply have to tough it out, live through it, and let nature take its course. The liver heals itself, you know."

To me, living through it meant working through it. I wanted to control the situation. But when I awoke on Monday morning, I realized that the hepatitis had taken control of me. All I could do was stay in bed and wait for healing. Just walking to the kitchen taxed me. Going to the office was out of the question. Never had I felt so helpless. For the first time in my adult life I was no longer in control. I couldn't go and get health.

Bill Fackler came by the house frequently to check my progress. For three months I remained in bed while Waights Henry and Dr. Toombs Kay, professor of religion at LaGrange College, held forth in the pulpit. Both were clergy colleagues of mine in the North Georgia Conference.

In the old days they referred to hepatitis as melancholia, and I began to understand why. The debilitating effects of the disease left me discouraged, even depressed—a state of mind I had never experienced. We had three children, and I regretted that they had to see me in such a state. I reached the point where I was feeling sorry for myself, fearful that I was going to develop cirrhosis of the liver. After two months Tuck and I agreed that we all needed a change, so she drove me to Atlanta to spend a week with my folks.

A sermon I had preached several years before came back to haunt me. It was about Elijah. He had won a momentous contest with the forces of Baal at Mount Carmel, enraging pagan Queen Jezebel. She was bent on revenge, and the prophet was fleeing from her wrath. He found refuge in a cave—alone.

The prophet had given up on goodness. Sitting there in a cave, weary and forlorn in his flight, he was ready to quit. To die, in fact. But in I Kings 19:9, God put the question straight to him: "What are you *doing* here, Elijah?" (emphasis mine) As a matter of fact, the premier prophet wasn't doing anything but indulging himself in morbid introspection. After all, one's perspective is severely limited looking out of the mouth of a cave. Elijah needed a different outlook—a new perspective. Stephen Covey, in *Seven Habits of Highly Effective People*, hits the nail on the head when he says that the way we see the problem *is* the problem. This was my problem—the way I was looking at it.

God uses various people to get our attention and give us new insight. In this case it was Lona Mae Rutledge, a godly woman who had come to work in our home when we first arrived in LaGrange. She was about sixty years old and full of wisdom. This modest African-American seldom spoke unless she was spoken to. She was cleaning the kitchen one morning as I was moping around the house in my bathrobe.

"Well, Lona Mae," I said, "I've been dragging around here for months now, and I'm getting awfully discouraged. I've been doing a lot of praying, and a lot of people have been doing a lot of praying, but I don't seem to be doing any better."

She did not look directly at me, but stopped what she was doing and said, "Reverend Jones, we've got to pray *believing*."

"Say that again Lona Mae," I insisted.

She said it again with emphasis, "We've got to pray believing."

She might as well have hit me over the head with a hammer. Those five words from that saintly woman struck such a chord, the impact was profound.

She wasn't finished. "We've got a song we sing that says, 'Take your burden to the Lord and *leave* it there.' "

I leaned back in my chair and said, "You know, Lona Mae, you're right on target."

I had been taking my burden to the Lord and then taking it right back—praying negatively instead of praying confidently. My praying was a form of pitying myself rather than trusting God. The problem was more in my mind than in my body.

That experience in the kitchen improved my outlook. My attitude was different. I had come to a moment of truth: Let God have control. Only recently I came across some sound advice: "If God is your copilot, you'd better change seats." That's precisely what I did that day. It made the difference.

Opening Doors

One thing about us United Methodists: We keep our clergy on the move. They're on the move daily with church and community matters. Then, on an average of every four years, we transfer them to other parishes. There's no law to that effect, and I wish the average stay was longer. Anyhow, a moving stream doesn't stagnate. I figure that Tuck's and my family together have given about 175 years in ministry through our denomination. That's five of us: her father and grandfather, my father, son, and me. This involved about 35 or 40 moves. Some military folk might think that's piddling, but I think it's above average.

Anyhow, in 1963 I was appointed to Saint Mark Methodist

Church on Peachtree Street in the heart of Atlanta, where I faced a unique challenge by way of Saint Mark's illustrious history as a bellwether congregation and its strategic location in the unsettling Sixties.

I was seated with Mayor Ivan Allen at a banquet one night and we began to talk about the status of our city. He was now in the thick of the civil rights struggle, and along with Police Chief Herbert Jenkins, was recognized nationally for his leadership in a "city too busy to hate." He admitted that five years earlier, when he was president of the Chamber of Commerce, if the white leadership of the community had responded positively and actively to our Ministers' Manifesto urging responsible desegregation of the schools, we could have brought about peaceful, constructive change without being forced to do so by demonstrations and picketing from pressure groups, and the sanctions of the federal government.

African-American students from the Atlanta University complex had been protesting their exclusion from restaurants and other public institutions all across Atlanta. In June 1963, when we arrived back in Atlanta after four years in LaGrange, they had begun kneel-ins at churches that excluded blacks from their worship services.

The Reverend Dr. Dow Kirkpatrick, pastor at Saint Mark from 1957 until eight months before my arrival, was one of our strongest advocates of justice and inclusiveness. He took a leading role in publishing the 1957 manifesto.

In a column for *The Atlanta Journal and Constitution* he

wrote, "Jesus Christ, in particular, invites His followers to a positive love for every man, which makes unchristian the kind of forced segregation which implies superiority and inferiority."

He was prepared to lead his congregation through the difficult decisions that lay ahead, but in a national chain of appointments at the highest level of the denomination, Dow became pastor of First Methodist Church in Evanston, Illinois, in October 1962. In the eight months between Dr. Kirkpatrick's departure and my arrival, retired Bishop Arthur J. Moore was made interim pastor at Saint Mark by presiding Bishop John Owen Smith. Bishop Moore had preached to people of color across the world, and he would not shut them away from a church where he was serving in his own country. So the door was open to all when I came on the scene.

Bishop Moore preached and presented me to the congregation at Saint Mark on June 23, 1963. We were celebrating Holy Communion, and one of the communicants was a black woman seated on the front row. After the service she asked for my signature on her bulletin. Apparently she was going to give it to the group sponsoring the kneel-ins to certify that she had worshiped and not simply gone into the narthex and picked up a bulletin. I signed it without hesitation and bade her welcome to any and all services.

We had no trouble from that day on, while across the street at First Baptist civil rights workers picketed every Sunday morning for over a year because African-Americans were refused entrance. The pastor, Dr. Roy McClain, who had been the catalyst for the manifestoes, was righteously indignant that his congregation would not heed his strong appeal for an open-door policy. He left a few years later with a broken heart and failing health.

Two years later a black person requested membership at Saint Mark. At that time, 1965, no white Methodist congregation in Atlanta had received an African-American into its membership.

One Sunday morning an Atlanta University student handed a card to an usher indicating he wanted to join our church. He could not participate in the Methodist church nearest the university, but was told he could get in at Saint Mark. He explained later that he and his family were part of a predominantly white Methodist congregation in Cincinnati, and ours was the type worship experience he felt most comfortable in.

I knew this was another moment of truth for me and my congregation. I had authority to allow this young man to join our church, and the *Discipline*, our book of faith and order, stated that I should. I would not abdicate, but neither did I want to dictate. What value would there be in his belonging to a congregation that had no part in his admission? Instead, I wanted at least the leadership to have a sense of ownership of this historic move.

"You'll be here after I'm gone," I told the staff-parish relations committee and the administrative board. "I want us all to share in this experience."

The staff-parish relations committee supported my decision and asked the administrative board to do the same. They knew I was going to accept the young man into membership and was only asking for their support.

The board was divided. Some thought it was "a setup"—the African-American student wasn't sincere and wanted to stir things up. The fact was that the man's minister in Cincinnati—a friend of mine, Dr. Emerson Colaw—said he was an outstanding young man from a staunch church family.

When the debate was most intense, our scoutmaster, Ed Mann, came forward. Ed was a rugged, blunt, matter-of-fact middle-ager in the construction business. You never knew what Ed would say.

"We have a bunch of kids in our Scout troop every week from all around the central city," he said. "Some of them are colored, but that doesn't make any difference to us. They're a welcome part of our troop.

"If we let dark-skinned boys into our Scouting program on weeknights, how can we keep dark-skinned people away from worship and Sunday school on the Sabbath? We ought to accept this young fellow as a member."

I could have hugged him, and did after the meeting. Ed opened some eyes and some minds that night on Peachtree Street, and that bellwether congregation took a further step toward being the church God would have it be. We lost a few members, but we gained in grace and in the favor of our Lord.

Saint Mark continues to be a church on the growing edge

thirty-five years later. It's being called "The Miracle on Peachtree Street." Under the leadership of Dr. Mike Cordle, Saint Mark has sought intentionally to involve persons in their immediate Midtown community, including many who are gay and lesbian. As a result, the congregation, which had dwindled to 300 or 400 with attendance of about 150, has grown to a membership of 1,500 and average attendance of 800 or more. Most old-timers at Saint Mark have welcomed members of the gay community. One said that if the church had not opened its doors to homosexual persons, they would be closing the doors soon because of dwindling numbers. At a recent Annual Conference session, Saint Mark was given the Evangelism Award and a standing ovation.

The United Methodist Church, along with other denominations and faith groups, recognizes that sexuality is God's good gift to all persons. While calling for the intelligent, responsible, and faithful expression of this gift, we recognize our limited understanding of its complexity and encourage the medical, theological, and social disciplines to work with the church in understanding human sexuality more completely. We affirm the sanctity of the marriage covenant between a man and a woman. At the same time, our *Book of Discipline* states:

> Homosexual persons no less than heterosexual persons are individuals of sacred worth. All persons need the ministry and guidance of the church in their struggles for human fulfillment, as well as the spiritual and emo-

tional care of the fellowship that enables reconciling relationships with God, with others, and with self.

Our denomination does not condone the practice of homosexuality, but we do believe that God's grace is available to all. We implore families and congregations not to reject or condemn their lesbian and gay members and friends, and urge them to be in ministry for and with all persons. Let us remember that we are all fallible, flawed personalities who sin and fall short of the glory of God. As we relate to homosexual persons and to one another in dealing with an issue that is not going away, may we do so with Christian grace, always praying for discernment and wisdom under the continuing guidance of God.

Taking the Cross into the Crowded Ways

Decatur High School invited me to speak at a banquet honoring the girls and boys basketball teams on the evening of April 4, 1968, and just as I was winding up my comments, someone burst into the hall and announced that Martin Luther King Jr. had been shot. As president of the Christian Council of Metropolitan Atlanta, which had sponsored the manifesto on race relations ten years earlier, I expected I would be asked to make a public statement. So instead of mixing and mingling with the crowd, which I always enjoy, I rushed out of the hall and drove quickly to the parsonage. When I got home I told Tuck what had happened and then took the telephone off the hook. I needed time to draw up a succinct statement.

Aubrey Morris of WSB radio called as soon as I replaced the receiver and said Elmo Ellis, manager of the station, wanted several of us clergy to gather around the mike and talk in an effort to keep the city as calm as possible. Dr. William Holmes Borders of Wheat Street Baptist Church, Dr. Harry Fifield of First Presbyterian Church, Rabbi Jacob Rothchild of The Temple, and I engaged in conversation over the air with Ellis and Morris from about 11 P.M. until 1 A.M.

I took my seventeen-year-old son, David, with me to experience firsthand part of that moment in history. Mayor Allen had already gone to the King home, and with a police escort had taken Coretta Scott King to the airport to fly to Memphis to be at her husband's side. When news came that Dr. King was dead, they took her back to her residence and kept vigil throughout the night for the family's security. A steady rain caused many to stay indoors who might have taken to the streets, as others had in cities across the land.

The next morning, Friday, April 5, I called a meeting of the executive committee of the Christian Council to prepare for a memorial service and issue a press release. In the statement we affirmed Dr. King's courageous leadership, bemoaned the assassination, expressed sympathy to the King family, called for renewed commitment to justice and equality for all, and urged everyone to exercise restraint and reconciliation in the current crisis.

The Atlanta Journal that afternoon wrote:

> Dr. Bevel Jones, president of the Christian Council of Metropolitan Atlanta and pastor of the First Methodist Church of Decatur, said Dr. King, by reason of his leadership in the civil rights cause, was himself the center of continuing controversy.
>
> "Thinking people are beginning to realize, however, the man was a catalyst, not the cause of the movement that has now become the major crisis in this country."
>
> Dr. Jones said the "revolution of rising expectations" is an inescapable phenomenon. The question is whether or not the objectives of human dignity, liberty and equality will be sought by rational and peaceful means—or whether extremisms and violence will prevail.
>
> "In a time that threatens the security as well as the sanity of our nation, all citizens—both white and black—should determine to practice more honestly the motto of the State of Georgia: Wisdom, Justice and Moderation," he urged.

In the meantime some of my colleagues in Memphis, the Reverend Joe Pennell (now bishop of the Richmond, Virginia area) the Reverend Frank McRae, and other clergy, were in the thick of the tumultuous aftermath of the assassination. The very next morning a company of them gathered at Saint Mary's Cathedral to march to city hall and implore Mayor Henry Loeb to heed the sanitation workers' appeal for more equitable compensation. It was on behalf of the sanitation workers, you may recall, that Dr. King went to Memphis.

As this group of clergy began their march, Dean Bill Dimmich called a halt and went back into the cathedral, returning with the processional cross. He held it high as he led the march. A woman in an apartment along the way came out and shouted, "Dean Dimmich, the cross belongs in the cathedral! Take the cross back to the cathedral!" Unperturbed, the procession went forward and made their appeal. Unfortunately it landed on deaf ears. Still, the clergy had witnessed to their faith and to the truth.

Our Lord didn't die within some comfortable chancel between two candlesticks. He died on a rugged hill between two thieves. There was no inspiring liturgy or stirring music when He breathed his last. It was amidst a maddening mob of misguided citizens clamoring for his blood, and callous soldiers gambling for his garment. Christ will not let us domesticate Him and keep Him within the secure confines of a sanctuary. He insists that we go with Him "where cross the crowded ways of life, where sound the cries of race and clan . . . in haunts of wretchedness and greed, on shadowed thresholds dark with fear . . ." (Frank Mason North)

Hippies and the Veneer of Society

Everything nailed down came loose in the 1960s. We had long since lost our innocence as a nation, and we were constrained by the younger generation to reconsider our values and culture as a society.

Before my appointment to Saint Mark Methodist Church, our family had been living in LaGrange, Georgia. David, our oldest, who was ten at the time, views those days as "Camelot." We were somewhat insulated by the easygoing style of a small town from the turmoil faced by cities across the country. But those days were not to last.

The Saint Mark parsonage was in the Ansley Park neighborhood, and my drive to work each day took me through a section of town full of young people coming to the metropolis seeking community and authentic relationships. It formed the nucleus of the hippie district—the Haight-Ashbury of the Southeast.

I had dropped David off at school one morning and was driving to the church when a young man stood by the curb with his thumb out. He looked to be in his late teens, and carried nothing but a book. I decided to offer my assistance.

I pulled over and opened the passenger door.

"Can I help you?" I asked.

"I'm going to Miami," he answered, "and need to get through town to I-75."

I told him to get in and I would take him to the church and see what we could do for him.

"What's your name?" I asked.

"Dino Mio," he said. It sounded like an alias.

We talked more, and he told me that his father was in prison and his mother had disappeared. He had slept the previous night in a used car lot up in Marietta.

I knew people who could help Dino Mio get a job and a place to stay, and I suggested that he remain in Atlanta, but he insisted that Miami was where he wanted to get established.

To make a long story short, we took care of his immediate needs, and I gave him a letter with a check made out to Dr. Dick Blanchard, pastor of Trinity Methodist Church in downtown Miami. I bought him a ticket at the bus station and sent him on his way with my blessing.

Dick wrote right away that he had gotten our mysterious friend a place to stay and would help get him a job. That was in October.

Now hear this! In February I called Dr. Paul Horton in Saint Petersburg to verify a couple from his church who were on the road and needed our help. He did so, then informed me that the preachers down his way were calling me "Smoky."

"Why Smoky?" I asked.

"Because of that young boy you sent to Dick Blanchard. Haven't you heard? He set two churches on fire, and was caught on New Year's Eve, the day before the Orange Bowl game, trying to set fire to Dick's own church."

Each of the fires had been started in the choir loft with leaves from hymn books. The book he had when I met him was a piano instruction book! I was dumbfounded.

Now for the rest of the story. One of the burned-out churches was White Temple Methodist Church, which sat diagonally across from Trinity Methodist Church. One had been a Northern Methodist congregation, thus their proximity. For years since the merger of the Methodist Churches of the South and North, Florida Conference leaders had tried to merge the two congregations. Nothing doing.

But when White Temple had no place to worship, Trinity invited their neighbors to worship with them. After a couple of months, they liked the arrangement so much they decided to make it permanent. They ended up uniting and moving down the street to a more strategic location, where they built a new facility and became an increasingly vital force in the heart of greater Miami.

God still works in mysterious ways, God's wonders to perform!

In our four years at Saint Mark, I came in contact with quite a number of young people like Dino Mio, lost and searching. They made me more keenly aware that the church must stay on the growing edge, continually relating its mission to the context in which it exists. Dr. Emil Brunner was right: "The church lives by its mission as a fire exists by burning."

Saint Mark owned a house on the street behind the church and used it as a gathering place for young people. We called it simply "The House." Here young adults from all over the Southeast experienced Christian fellowship without the ecclesial trappings that might have been foreboding to them. It was a time of challenge and innovation, to say the least. Our efforts gave impetus to the larger urban ministry of Methodism in Atlanta.

I perceived that in a crass and often grotesque way, the hippies, by and large, were trying to get behind the veneer of conventional society—beneath the superficial and the artificial—to what is real and substantive. They espoused the love of people rather than things. I saw in many hippies a genuine love for one another, though their conduct was often misguided. In unconventional and, at times, unacceptable ways, they seemed to be saying, "Every individual is special. Your value is not in what you wear, your station in life, or what you achieve. It's who you are as a person."

The 1960s spawned the renewalist movement in the church. Making the church relevant was the order of the day. "Let the world write the agenda" became the watchword among radical reformers. The pendulum then swung too far in the direction of the secularization of the gospel. We were loosed from our theological moorings. Neglecting the devotional life and corporate worship, many social activists got disillusioned or burned out.

Nonetheless, through civil rights, the hippies, and the Vietnam War, the church rediscovered itself and in no small measure underwent creative change and spiritual growth.

From Generation to Generation

As our son David left for college, I reminded him of the maxim I had found so helpful: "Not dead center, but the dynamic middle." Campus life and national upheaval soon provided him the challenge to function accordingly.

I still have in my file the following letter, which David wrote to me as a pre-ministerial student at Birmingham Southern College in May 1970. A month earlier President Nixon had ordered the invasion of Cambodia, and on May 4, four student protesters at Kent State University had been shot and killed by National Guardsmen.

> Some of the students held a rally today in memory
> of the four students that were killed at Kent. This group

then decided that it was their prerogative to lower the flag to half-staff in memory of the students and as an expression of sorrow at the action that Nixon had taken. For the rest of the day the flag went up and down depending on who happened to walk by and what their feeling was. It was ridiculous in one sense. But it was tragic in another because of how lightly both sides were treating the symbol of our country.

Toward the end of discussion tonight, talk about the flag incident led to talk about the college situation in general. Finally, one girl said, "Why don't you come out and use the word—*revolution*. It's not a question of when and where it's coming, only what side you will be on."

Now how in the world am I supposed to be able to calmly continue my studies when part of the students feel that way and the other extreme is taking the "My country, right or wrong" bit?

Reports throughout the nation indicate widespread unrest, and the possibility of a student rebellion seems real. An article in one of our religious periodicals lifts up a fellow who can moderate between the extremes as the new type of hero. My friend John and I are trying to play the reconciling role.

But there just doesn't seem to be anything we can do, even to the point of not being able to get people to listen to reason. Some people that I've tried to convince to cool it till they get the facts say they don't have to wait on the facts.

What people like us need to know is, who are we supposed to look to? When will more of the reasonable community and political leaders find a way to communicate with young people?

Well, I just thought I'd spout off some of my frustrations. Any advice is really appreciated!

P.S. What's the church supposed to be doing?

I responded:

Our country appears to be torn asunder at this juncture in history. Everybody is confused and admittedly we are playing a great deal of it by ear. There's so much hysteria, and as always in a crisis, many mistake adrenaline for courage. Then there are those who have a chronic messianic complex. They inevitably move to the front of the stage at a time like this.

Extremism is the order of the day. If you aren't decidedly to the left or the right, you just aren't with it. The true moderates are accused of cowardice and compromise. They are maligned for not taking a stand. This is admittedly a danger. But maybe some of us apparent fence-straddlers are put here to keep those who think all the truth is in on their side from tilting the world off its axis.

How better can responsible Christians serve their

fellows than by reconciling extremes in a free society? It's hard, because you get it from both sides. And sometimes it's quite lonely in the middle with the legions running off like wild horses to the right or the left.

If it is any consolation to you, I am building my expectations of a bright future on the belief that there is a solid, decent, dependable core of dedicated people in this world who are going to pull us through this glorious mess. God has never left Himself without them. And most important of all, I believe God is in this human predicament working out a great purpose in and through all who remain faithful to Him.

P.S. As for the church: One of our primary roles is to do all we can to reconcile differences and resolve problems constructively.

The Ultimate Accolade

For all of her adult life, my mother loved England the way Stephen Foster loved the Suwannee River. Foster never saw the Suwannee before he wrote "That's where my heart is turning ever . . ." Mother had never visited England, but she was well versed in English history and literature. She enjoyed following the activities of the royal family in a time when the Windsors were almost universally respected.

So in 1972, I urged her and her younger sister, Imogene, to go on a tour of England sponsored by Wesleyan College. Mother was always concerned about Dad's health, and catered to his physical needs meticulously. He was now eighty-two, and she felt he might run into trouble if she was away for two weeks.

Tuck and I assured her we would have Dad stay with us, and we would take care of him. Dad agreed, and she reluctantly set sail.

Things went well for the first two days, then Dad complained of acute indigestion. We went to church at Decatur First for supper, and afterward, a beautiful choral presentation in the sanctuary. When we got home from church, his condition grew worse. The next morning we took him to Emory Hospital and learned that he was experiencing congestive heart failure. The doctor could not give us a specific prognosis, but we knew it was very serious. We debated whether to contact Mother. She and Imogene were due home in a week. Our doctor agreed that telling her from such a distance of Dad's illness might be too much for her. We would wait it out. Annual Conference was in session across the campus at Glenn Memorial Church. I went from the Conference to the hospital continually throughout the week. Bishop John Owen Smith led the assembly in prayer for Dad, and we sang the old gospel favorite, "My Faith Is Built." Never before had that chorus meant quite so much to me.

> On Christ, the solid rock, I stand
> All other ground is sinking sand.

Mother and Imogene came home on Saturday, and I picked them up at the airport. Mother talked enthusiastically about the trip, and I waited until we got to her house before I told her about Dad. Then I informed her of his condition, and she went to pieces.

"I told you this would happen!" she cried.

"Mother," I said, "the doctor assured us that this had nothing to do with his diet or his care." But I don't think she heard anything I said. She never mentioned her trip to England again as long as she lived.

It was tough for her to go to the hospital. Dad became weaker, and I was in deep distress. When I told him Mother and Imogene were safely home, he smiled and said, "Everything's all right now." He no doubt had been more anxious about her than I realized, and she about him.

I wrote in my journal how serene and steadfast Dad was during what he must have known were his last days. All the nurses talked about how gracious, gentle, and kind he was. He handled dying with grace and dignity. He died on Sunday at daybreak. Milo Hamilton, a cherished friend and Voice of the Atlanta Braves, got the word and graciously announced Dad's death, expressing his sympathy while broadcasting the game that afternoon. We began hearing from friends and colleagues from far and near.

Bishop Arthur J. Moore, who had been aware of Dad's condition, had agreed to officiate at his funeral. When Dad died the bishop was at Lake Junaluska, where he would preach at the Southeastern Jurisdictional Conference of the Methodist Church two days later. Our son David, then a college student, was working at the Lake Junaluska Assembly that summer, so he and Bishop Moore flew down together for the service. David said that while they waited for a driver to take them to the airport, the bishop, beginning what was to be the next-to-last year of his life, said, "I'm an old man now, and I've traveled all over the world and met many people. I've discovered that while it's fine to be a great man, it's even better to be a good man.

"Your grandfather Jones wasn't a great man, but he was a good man. Somewhere along the way we've lost that reality."

The service was one of celebration with a full sanctuary at Audubon Forest Methodist Church, where I was the founding pastor at the beginning of my ministry, and where Dad had served as minister of visitation since his retirement. The two colleagues who succeeded me at Audubon Forest, the Reverend Dwight Nysewander and the Reverend Wallace Wiggins, offered their tributes and words of comfort. Bishop Moore, who had been Dad's bishop for twenty years, spoke of Dad's "quiet courage." The bishop was a powerful preacher, and he was at his best that day in proclaiming our faith in God's steadfast love and life eternal.

As my family and I walked out of the church, I said to them, "At the altar of this church for ten years, I asked people to come and make their commitment, whether it was their tithes and offerings, the sacrament of the Lord's Supper, baptism, membership in the church, or holy wedlock. If we cannot now commit Dad in death to God in the assurance of his everlasting well-being, all these other commitments are suspect."

I felt then, and I still feel, as if Dad in a way sort of crawled inside of me. The communion of the saints became more real

than ever. Each year at the memorial services at both the Annual Conference and the Council of Bishops, when we sing
"For All the Saints," I think especially of my father.

> For all the saints, who from their labors rest,
> Who Thee by faith before the world confessed.
> Thy name, O Jesus, be forever blest.
>
> Thou was their rock, their fortress and their might;
> Thou, Lord, their captain in the well-fought fight;
> Thou, in the darkness drear, their one true light.
>
> O may thy soldiers, faithful, true, and bold,
> Fight as the saints who nobly fought of old,
> And win with them the victor's crown of gold.
>
> O blest communion, fellowship divine!
> We feebly struggle, they in glory shine;
> Yet all are one in thee, for all are thine.
>
> And when the strife is fierce, the warfare long,
> Steals on the ear the distant triumph song,
> And hearts are brave again, and arms are strong.
>
> From earth's wide bounds, from ocean's farthest coast,
> Through gates of pearl streams in the countless host,
> Singing to Father, Son, and Holy Ghost,
> Alleluia, Alleluia.

The Anguish of Alzheimer's

In the months and years following Dad's death, I would look back on that trip from the airport with Mother to her house, and her difficulty dealing with Dad's illness and death, and see the first signs of Alzheimer's, which would eventually hold her in its grip for almost a decade until her death at age eighty-six.

Bit by bit, she showed signs of mental deterioration, and the things she once knew slowly faded away. In the early stages of the disease, she lived alone and continued to go to church and teach. On special occasions or outings with the family she functioned quite normally. Gradually the connections began to fail.

We moved her to Wesley Woods retirement community and eventually to the nursing home. Whenever I visited her, I did just what the experts now say not to do, asking her the names of the grandchildren, then answering for her, trying to cram all that information back into her brain. But it wouldn't work. Instead of asking her questions, I learned simply to rehearse some of the key persons and places she held dearest. Long after names and places ceased to register, I would quote familiar Bible passages, especially the Psalms. Then I would hover over her and sing softly some of the old hymns. Sometimes there would be a faint glimmer of recognition. What mattered most was simply being in each other's presence and hoping somehow she knew of my love. It was indeed, as Nancy Reagan says, a "long goodbye."

Eventually I had to accept the fact that my mother, who had brought me into the world, nurtured me as a child, guided me through my teens, and encouraged me as an adult, was apparently unaware of who she was.

I was glad Dad did not live to see his beloved Gertrude in the throes of this demonic affliction. I cannot imagine anything more devastating. In the book of Daniel, there is an apocalyptic term, the abomination of desolation (12:11). It is reiterated in Matthew and Mark. It is an apt description of Alzheimer's. By destroying the brain, Alzheimer's robs the victim of his or her sense of personhood, of one's own identity. It is indeed an abomination of desolation.

I agonized over it and often asked myself the question,

"Where is my mother?"

The only peace I found was in the confidence that she was in the eternal embrace of a loving God. I had used Paul's great statement in Romans many times in sermons and especially in services of death and resurrection. Now it was exceedingly personal and sure solace for my troubled soul.

> What then are we to say about these things? If God is for us, who is against us? Who will separate us from the love of Christ? Will hardship, or distress, or persecution, or famine, or nakedness, or peril, or sword? . . .
>
> No, in all these things we are more than conquerors through him who loved us. For I am convinced that neither death, nor life, nor angels, nor rulers, nor things present, nor things to come, nor powers, nor height, nor depth, nor anything else in all creation, will be able to separate us from the love of God in Christ Jesus our Lord. (Romans 8:31, 35, 37-39)

Mother died on November 14, 1985, and her body was laid to rest by my father's in West View Cemetery, Atlanta. Dying was "sweet release" from her tortured mind. Death and resurrection are the ultimate cure for all that ails us. There's validity in the words of an old hymn, "Earth has no sorrow that heaven cannot heal."

Advice from a Prince of the Pulpit

One Sunday morning during my years as a college upper-classman, I was fooling with the radio when I heard a magnificent voice resonating across the air. I stopped turning the knob for a moment to listen. The man obviously was a preacher, and a superb one. I continued to listen, not only to hear what he had to say, but to learn who he was. At the end of the sermon an announcer said, "You have been listening to Dr. Ralph W. Sockman on the National Radio Pulpit from New York City."

I had seen the name Sockman on several books in our home, and was determined to learn more about him. I read the books and made it a habit to listen to Dr. Sockman whenever possible. He came on the radio at 10 o'clock on Sunday morning, so I would sometimes slip out to the car during the Sunday school hour and tune in.

Then a year or so after I graduated from seminary and was serving my first church in southwest Atlanta, Dr. Sockman was the speaker for Ministers Week at Emory. I was going to get to meet him in person!

When the week arrived, I drove over to Emory and found a seat up front in Glenn Memorial Sanctuary. The place was jammed with pastors from all over the South, as well as lay people who had come to know Dr. Sockman over the radio. He finished his sermon, and I waited until the crowd around him dispersed so we could chat for a moment. I told him how I had listened to him so eagerly over the radio and had read some of his books. Then I rather timidly asked if it would be possible for us to spend a few minutes together. To my joy, he said, "Sure, young man. Come over and have breakfast with me in the morning."

I could hardly sleep that night, and at the dawn's early light I hastened across town. When I knocked on his door, Dr. Sockman answered wearing his pants, socks, and a t-shirt, with shaving lather covering his face. You could have bowled me over with a feather!

"Come on in," he said. "Make yourself at home while I finish getting ready."

Inside, a pipe smoldered, and I knew I was engaged in one of the great experiences of my life, just being in the same room with this icon while he prepared for the day. I had dreamed of getting to know Ralph Sockman, and here he was, half dressed, and having to shave like me and other mortals. We went to breakfast, and I asked him every question I could think of about preaching and leading a congregation.

Twelve years later, as president of the Southeastern Jurisdictional Ministers' Conference at Lake Junaluska, I had the privilege of inviting Dr. Sockman to preach that week and presenting him to an auditorium full of clergy. We had several opportunities to visit one-on-one and deepen our friendship. Then in 1968 I had him as the first in a succession of great pulpiteers during my nine-year pastorate at Decatur First United Methodist: Bishop Gerald Kennedy; Bishop Robert Goodrich; Bishop Kenneth Goodson; Dr. Ernest Campbell; and Dr. Chet Pennington.

The last night Dr. Sockman was in town, we had him for dinner at the parsonage, and the next morning I drove him to the airport. It was the last time I would be with him. He was nearly eighty, and died a year or so later.

He reminded me how important the pastorate is; he was pastor of Christ Church in New York for over forty years—his only pastorate. In his prime, the Northeastern Jurisdictional Conference was in the process of electing him bishop. He withdrew from the balloting, stating that he felt his calling was to the parish. As we were bidding each other goodbye, he said good-naturedly, "Don't let 'em make a bishop out of you!"

The Preacher Everybody Knows

Before Billy Graham arrived for his first Atlanta crusade half a century ago, the newspapers hit him with rumors and innuendoes. In 1950 the prevailing image of traveling evangelists was Elmer Gantry, from the Sinclair Lewis novel, who breezed into cities, fleeced the flocks, then breezed out again with bulging pockets.

Dr. Graham, thirty-one years old, was just becoming known. He acknowledged, "We know that the matter of finances has been a stigma in evangelism campaigns for a long time." He pledged to have the finances audited at the end of the crusade, with copies of the results sent to local ministers and newspapers.

The questions and rumors persisted, including one that Dr. Graham would be guaranteed $100,000 to come to Atlanta. At that point Bishop Arthur J. Moore, of the North Georgia Conference of the Methodist Church, spoke out in support of Billy Graham. Bishop Moore himself was world renowned as an evangelist, and was highly regarded in Atlanta. He said in effect, "I know Billy Graham. I have watched him develop, and I know his integrity. He can be trusted with fiscal affairs. I welcome him to this city, and I want you to."

Bishop Moore joined the local committee organizing the event in a public effort to cement support for Billy Graham, and he sat on the front row at Ponce de Leon Ball Park on opening night of the six-week Crusade alongside Dr. Pierce Harris and Dr. Charles Allen, ministers of two of the city's largest Methodist congregations.

As a twenty-four-year-old theology school graduate serving my first parish, I sat nowhere near the front row, although my growing congregation and I supported the crusade with our attendance. Many thousands more Atlantans also attended—496,600 over six weeks. In his autobiography, *Just As I Am*, Billy Graham describes Bishop Moore as a "staunch supporter of the Crusade."

Twenty-three years later the Christian Council of Metropolitan Atlanta invited Dr. Graham for a return engagement, a weeklong crusade at Atlanta-Fulton County Stadium. I was asked to serve as clergy chairman of the Crusade Committee, and Tom Cousins, a devout Presbyterian and prominent developer, served as lay chairman.

One of the keys to the success of Billy Graham Crusades is the full year of preparation in the host city. Tom and I worked with Dr. Graham's point person, Henry Holley, in coordinating music and transportation, deciding which key civic and religious leaders would sit on stage each night, and worked out details with Atlanta Stadium. Security was critical because the Black Panthers had come to town, and their tactic of strident confrontation was a threat. Isn't it sad to have to be defensive in a religious undertaking?

Everything went smoothly, however, until just days before the Crusade was to begin. MARTA employees went on strike, virtually shutting down the city's public transportation system.

Tom and I called on churches that had bus ministries to help us get people to and from the stadium. Most of them gladly cooperated. A few, however, emphatically declined, insisting that they could not participate because Dr. Graham was too liberal.

Tom was flabbergasted. "My soul," he said, "if they look on Billy Graham as liberal, they're in the religious backwoods."

When Dr. Graham arrived in Atlanta, he asked if I could arrange a visit with Bishop Moore. He remembered how the bishop had affirmed his ministry before the world knew much about Billy Graham. Dr. Graham never forgot that favor or betrayed that trust.

Bishop Moore suggested that I bring Dr. Graham to his

house for breakfast and include Dr. William R. Cannon, then dean of the Candler School of Theology. I picked up Dr. Graham at his hotel and drove to Bishop Moore's home near Emory, where we were met at the door by Blanche, a dear old African-American woman who had been in his home for more than thirty years. She led us to a big mahogany table, where we spent the next three hours enjoying a four-course breakfast Blanche prepared and served. (Mrs. Moore was deceased.)

While we savored ham, eggs, grits, gravy, toast, biscuits, fruit, juice, and hot coffee, we covered the waterfront from cities in the U.S. and in faraway lands as Graham and Moore compared preaching missions the world over. Dr. Cannon, brilliant church historian and theologian who himself had traveled extensively, was a leader in the World Methodist Council, and was much involved in Methodist dialogue with the Vatican, participated enthusiastically in the conversation, especially on matters of doctrine. It was indeed a rare and rich experience.

Several months later Dr. Cannon and I were called to the bishop's home by his daughter-in-law, Mrs. Wordlaw Moore (Linda). The old bishop was in the throes of acute anxiety, tossing in his bed and calling the names of cities all over the world. In his travail he apparently thought he was in captivity. He had asked Linda to call Bishop Cannon and me to come and help him. We rushed over, went to his bedside, and calmed him down as best we could. But the bishop was still in deep distress. Again he called the names of many cities. Then his eyes focused sharply on us as he relaxed, and whispered, "The ultimate supremacy of righteousness."

Again came the recital of cities in far-off lands, and then faintly the reassuring refrain, "The ultimate supremacy of righteousness." We learned later that the bishop was suffering minor strokes. Still, in his disorientation, his addled mind came to focus on that fundamental tenet of his indomitable faith.

What a dramatic illustration of the faith that sustains us! How often in our weariness we give way to perplexity and fear. Then in the deep recesses of the soul comes the peace that passes understanding and the assurance of God's providential care and sustaining grace.

I presided over Bishop Moore's funeral a few months later at Glenn Memorial Church on the Emory campus. Dr. Louie D. Newton, beloved pastor of Druid Hills Baptist Church, Bishop Cannon, and Bishop Nolan Harmon were the principal speakers. The service was one of celebration and hope, praising God for Bishop Moore's amazing ministry.

When I became bishop of the Western North Carolina Conference a decade later, Billy and Ruth Graham welcomed me in their home in Montreat, the Presbyterian conference center in Black Mountain, North Carolina. We spent a cold February Saturday afternoon sitting around the fireplace deepening our friendship, recalling rich experiences, and reflecting on life and faith.

The next morning I preached at the United Methodist Church in Black Mountain, and Dr. Graham worshiped with us. The people were more excited about his presence than mine. I understood their sentiments. I too was quite awed.

One of the last roles I played before retiring from North Carolina was helping launch what we thought at the time might be Dr. Graham's last Crusade. I offered the opening prayer in Ericcson Stadium, home of the Carolina Panthers pro football team in Charlotte, Dr. Graham's hometown. What a privilege to know this man who has been personal friends with every president since Eisenhower, as well as leaders the world over, preached to more than 200 million people, and led multitudes into a relationship with the living Christ.

In a day when the word *televangelism* arouses suspicion, Billy Graham has been exemplary and has kept the public's confidence. His services from the beginning have been open to everyone; he maintains impeccable fiscal and moral integrity; he never disparages other clergy or any religious group; he is not a shill for any denomination; he urges converts to become active in a local church; and he is sincere when he gives God the glory.

The Difference You Make

In the 1970s, when I had the opportunity to visit with best-selling author James Michener, I asked him what he would emphasize if he were in the pulpit in modern America. He tugged the sleeve of my shirt and said, "This cloth is no better than the individual threads that comprise it. The same is true of society. It is no better than the individuals who make it up. I would emphasize that everybody counts; everybody makes a difference. No matter our rank or station, each of us should be the best that we can be." Then Michener hit the jugular vein by insisting that everyone, upon reaching young adulthood, ought to have made a commitment to the common good.

Former United States Senator George Mitchell of Maine

made one of the shortest commencement speeches on record—
six minutes—at Emory University in 2000. He echoed what
Michener had stressed, emphasizing that real fulfillment in
life comes from striving for an objective that is "larger than
self-interest." Then he reinforced his point with a quote from
John Gardner:

> An excellent plumber is infinitely more admirable
> than an incompetent philosopher. The society which
> scorns excellence in plumbing because it is a humble
> activity, and tolerates mediocrity in philosophy because
> it is an exalted activity, will have neither good plumbing
> nor good philosophy. Neither its pipes nor its theories
> will hold water.

One of the basic principles of the Hebrew/Christian tradition is the sacredness of all vocations. A vocation is far more
than a mere occupation. It roots in a Latin word meaning "a
call or summons." Such a life isn't primarily concerned about
making a living, but making a contribution, being part of the
answer rather than part of the problem.

I like the way another of the great minds of our time,
Bernaro Overstreet, puts it:

> You say the little efforts that I make
> Will do no good.
> They will never pevail to tip the hovering scale

Where justice hangs in the balance.
I don't think
I ever really thought they would.
But I am prejudiced beyond debate
In favor of my right to choose which side
Shall feel the stubborn ounces of my weight.

When our oldest child, David, accepted the call to ordained ministry, our second-born, Mark, quipped, "Well, that takes care of this generation." Yet in his own right, and in his own way, Mark is ministering through teaching. He is a fine artist and shares that talent with high school students seeking a vocation themselves. In a recent presentation, Mark said he has always had a desire to serve others and make a difference in people's lives. "I am convinced I'm in this business for a greater purpose than just training students for the graphics industry. My primary goal is to build the self-esteem and confidence needed to interact with society, and to further worthy values." He concluded by saying he has found his purpose in life.

That same kind of summons has shaped our daughter's life and work. Henry and Carolyn McDowell came at my bidding to Decatur First Church in the fall of 1971, to direct the ministry of music and drama. They did wonders for our parish and are now in their thirtieth year—and counting! They turned our young teenager, Sharon, on like a Christmas tree. So captivated was she by theatrics, she felt compelled to devote her life to the performing arts. I thrilled at her performance in productions at the church, but I did not envision her making a profession of it. I called to her attention numerous other fields of endeavor, but she was hooked. Finally one day as we were discussing her future, she laid one on me: "Dad, I feel called to drama as surely as you do to ordained ministry."

That disarmed me completely. I yielded humbly and have found deep satisfaction in her fulfillment of an innate talent and consuming passion. She is now director of education for Atlanta's Alliance Theatre Company and goes about it with gusto and a genuine sense of stewardship. Not only are she and her colleagues relating drama to real life and developing talent, they use drama as an outreach to people who may experience theatre for the first time. Sharon has learned what Frederick Buechner advocates: "Your vocation is where your deep joy and the world's deep hunger meet."

One of the greatest examples of vocation is former President Jimmy Carter and his wife, Rosalynn. I have known this wonderful couple since he was governor of Georgia. Many of us feel that President Carter made of the White House a stepping stone to greater things. As a former trustee of the Carter Center and a current member of its board of councillors, I know firsthand the magnificent service he and Mrs. Carter are rendering at home and abroad. Instead of resting on their laurels and taking it easy in their retirement years, the Carters are seeking throughout the world to prevent and resolve conflicts, enhance freedom and democracy, and improve health. They work alongside earth's forgotten people—those who are the most in need. They believe that individuals, given access to the necessary knowledge and resources, can change their lives and communities.

Millard Fuller, founder of Habitat for Humanity, tells of a poor woman working with a group of volunteers, including President Carter, building a home for her. On a sultry day in July, perspiration was dropping from President Carter's forehead into the cement he was mixing. She told Mr. Fuller how overwhelmed she was when she realized that the mortar in her house would contain sweat from the brow of a former president of the United States!

On a three-by-five card in my Bible is a quotation I have carried for decades. It is by Dr. Paul Sherer, great preacher of a couple of generations ago, in his book, *Love Is a Spendthrift*:

> The fundamental joy of being a Christian consists not of being good. I get tired of that. But in standing with God against some darkness or some void and watching the light come . . . The joy of religion is in having your fling, by the mercies of God, at shaping where you are, as a potter shapes a vase, one corner of His eternal kingdom.

Aunt Pearl and Amazing Grace

In 1976 Bishop William R. Cannon placed me at First United Methodist Church in Athens, the city of my childhood. I loved Athens, but I didn't want to leave Atlanta. I had become so accustomed to metropolitan life, it took me a year and a half to gear down to the slower pace. I had just turned fifty, and Sharon, our youngest, was going off to college, leaving Tuck and me with an empty nest. The change turned out to be a blessing, and I got to know myself, and Tuck, better. As we grow older we begin to realize life is lived in chapters. Somewhere I came across this delineation of the scale of life: tender teens, teachable twenties, tireless thirties, fiery forties, fervent fifties, silvery sixties, saintly seventies, aching eighties, needy nineties. Right on target, I've found.

My "second coming" to Athens was one of spiritual growth and rich relationships. There I enjoyed the intellectual atmosphere surrounding the University of Georgia, the stimulus of student life, association with lifelong friends, and, of course, college athletics.

Dominique Wilkins and Hershel Walker were dominating the basketball court and the gridiron. As chaplain of the golf team, I got to know future professionals such as Chip Beck. When I played with them during practice rounds, they felt like praying for me instead of me praying for them. I have found, however, that prayer on the golf course doesn't do any good if you don't swing the club right!

Bishop Cannon, himself a University of Georgia graduate, saw Athens First Church as the most strategic Methodist pulpit in Georgia. The gospel is amplified in any educational setting through prominent educators who are already leaders and many students who will be the leaders of tomorrow. To this day I frequently encounter middle-aged men and women who talk about attending the University of Georgia when I was pastor there and what the church meant to them.

After about a year I was acclimated and very much at home in the "Classic City." Mother's dementia worsened, and we brought her from Wesley Woods retirement community to a nursing home in Athens—a transition she was hardly aware of.

In the midst of all this came the election of lay and clergy delegates to the 1980 session of the General and Jurisdictional Conferences of the United Methodist Church. The clergy delegate with the most votes each quadriennium customarily becomes the Annual Conference's nominee for bishop. That was the case in 1979. Dr. Cecil Myers, pastor of Peachtree Road United Methodist Church in Atlanta, and my immediate predecessor at First Church Athens, led the balloting. I was second. The delegation chose him as our candidate, and I returned to Athens confident that he had a good chance, and we were wholeheartedly behind him.

Then Dr. Myers surprisingly informed us in November that he was withdrawing because of physical problems. In two weeks the delegation would meet in Atlanta to choose a replacement. As the second person in the balloting. I knew I might be chosen, and I wasn't prepared for this eventuality. I wasn't sure the bishopric was for me, or that I was ready for it, though I had aspirations for it. The words of Dr. Ralph Sockman haunted me: "Don't let 'em make a bishop out of you!" I spent those two weeks in earnest prayer and reflection. My only viable approach was to trust the collective mind of the delegation.

As it turned out, a dear friend of mine got the nod. I must confess feelings of both disappointment and relief. I congratulated the nominee and assured him of my continued friendship and loyal support. Then I plunged back into my work at Athens First Church, shaken, but confident that things would turn out for the good of all concerned.

Dad was deceased, and Mother was no longer capable of comprehending such matters, so I decided to drive over to visit her oldest sister, Pearl, who was in a nursing home in Commerce.

Mother and five of her six siblings all left their rural homestead in the early part of the twentieth century, scattering across the United States. All except Aunt Pearl, who, by circumstance and disposition stayed near the old home place.

Aunt Pearl married a local farm boy, Albert Segars, and they made do with no electricity and no running water on a two-horse farm out from Maysville.

Uncle Albert died when their son and daughter were teenagers, and Aunt Pearl never married again. Instead she gritted her teeth, mustered up all the courage she could, and managed that farm. She had a hard row to hoe—literally. I visited the farm for a couple of weeks each summer, and saw her do manual labor that not just any man, and few women, could handle. Her life revolved around Hickory Flat Methodist Church. She was respected by all who knew her as a woman of wisdom and compassion. At age eighty-eight she was the victim of crippling arthritis.

When I arrived at the nursing home late in the afternoon, Aunt Pearl was propped up in bed with her favorite meal, cornbread and milk in a glass, on the tray pressed against her breast. We greeted each other affectionately, and she awkwardly resumed eating those spoonfuls of cornbread and milk.

"Aunt Pearl, can I help you with that?" I asked.

"Don't mind if you do," she replied.

I scooped out the white mush and put it into her mouth. Every once in a while she licked her lips.

"Aunt Pearl, you like this stuff, don't you?"

"I love it. Don't you want some?"

"You know I don't eat that kind of food," I said.

She stopped eating and with a devilish look in her eye said, "That's why your head is bald too!"

I reared back and laughed. That was typical of her unfailing sense of humor. She was a favorite aunt, righteous but not sanctimonious. We exchanged a few good stories, then I told her what had happened in the delegation and the mixed feelings I was experiencing.

She didn't ask a lot of questions about my situation. She just stopped for a moment as I held the spoon in front of her and said, "Bev, when you live as long as I have, you'll find that something other than your disappointments will kill you."

I put the spoon down in the glass and thought about that. This great soul who had endured more than her share of hard knocks and heartache, and whose faith was like the Rock of Gibralter, had put me back on course. It was truly a word in season.

I helped her finish the last few bites, and it was time for me to go back home. Before I left we joined in prayer.

I took her gnarled hand and started praying. When I finished, she began to pray as naturally as she'd been talking with me.

Now, I used to think as a kid that if I opened my eyes during a prayer I might be struck by lightning, and I still am uncomfortable with my eyes open in prayer. But I opened them during this one. I wanted to get the full benefit of it. Aunt Pearl's eyes were tightly closed, and that silver-white hair looked like a wreath around her weather-worn face. The longer she prayed, the tighter she clasped my hand and closed her eyes. She thanked the Lord for His guiding hand and sustaining presence, and rejoiced in what the church had meant to her and her family. Across the back roads of my mind as she prayed came the words of the third stanza of the old hymn "Amazing Grace":

> Through many dangers, toils, and snares,
> I have already come.
> 'Tis grace hath brought me safe thus far,
> And grace will lead me home.

I kissed her goodbye, rejoicing in the benediction I had received from one of God's saints, and walking with firmer tread.

Strength in Our Weakness

In July 1983 I became the nominee of the North Georgia Conference for bishop in the election that would take place at the Southeastern Jurisdictional Conference at Lake Junaluska the following year. I was overcome with gratitude for the honor of representing my home Conference and that of my father and son. The confidence my own people were placing in me was gratifying and humbling. The delegation, headed by lay leader Bob Martin, gave me strong support. Dr. Bill McKoy, my former associate at Decatur First United Methodist Church, worked diligently as our liaison with the other delegations.

The bishopric in the Methodist Church is the ecclesiastical zenith, in purely professional terms. There is something rather awesome about it, but nothing ultimate. It is not a separate order, but an office in which an elder is consecrated, i.e., set apart for a ministry of oversight and supervision.

I had aspirations of being a bishop, but I relished the pastorate and congregational life. I was only in my second year at Northside United Methodist Church, a growing congregation strategically located and abounding in talent, leadership, and resources. I felt good about the prospect of developing that parish and reaching out with them to bring the mind of Christ to bear redemptively upon the life of metropolitan Atlanta and beyond.

I had never served in an administrative position per se, not even the district superintendency. The nitty gritty of management is not my strength. The bishopric is heavy with "administrivia" and major decisions affecting many persons. The concern that I might be less than effective weighed ponderously on me. I became overanxious, and began to see the bishopric as larger than life.

In one of my previous congregations, a friend who was a pilot with Delta Airlines for twenty years shared with me the trauma he was undergoing as the company converted from propellers to jet propulsion. The change was forcing him out of his comfort zone, and almost defeated him. With prayer, encouragement, and determination, he worked through the transition and fulfilled his career admirably. I now found myself going through the same kind of experience.

John Wesley grappled with what he called "the sin of fear."

It can overtake any of us. Whereas stepping into the pulpit was always the height of excitement for me, I had reached the point where I sometimes stood at the door of the chancel as the organ sounded forth, wondering if I would get through another sermon. I became like Mark Wohlers, the ace relief pitcher for the Atlanta Braves who in 1998 suddenly lost his confidence and could not find the plate.

In such times we resort to that one true human refuge—another person's heart. Former NFL All-Pro center Bill Curry was head football coach at Georgia Tech and a member of Northside Church. We had been friends since his playing days at Tech, and were both intensely active in the Fellowship of Christian Athletes. I was his pastor at Saint Mark Church when he played pro ball. Now our roles reversed. He became my counselor and spiritual director.

Bill was an unfailing source of strength and guidance—a rock in a weary land. I have always urged my clergy colleagues and my students at Candler School of Theology to have a support group. All of us need all the help we can get. There come times when we need the faith of intimate friends and loved ones to bolster our own faith.

Of course, Tuck supported me as no one else could. For weeks she saw me wrestle with anxiety and self-doubt. It was my habit to get up early in the morning and enjoy a period of meditation while I prepared and ate my breakfast. Tuck began leaving inspirational material on the table each night for me to discover alone the next morning. It might be quotes, poetry, or scriptural passages, along with prayers.

One night I rolled and tossed and determined not to go through with the nomination. When I went to the kitchen table the next morning, Tuck's message was a prayer from John Baillie's classic *A Diary of Private Prayer*:

Almighty God . . . let me now go forth into the world with a brave and trustful heart. It has pleased Thee to withhold from me a perfect knowledge; therefore deny me not the grace of faith by which I may lay hold of things unseen. Thou hast given me little power to mold things to my own desire; therefore use Thine own omnipotence to bring Thy desires to pass within me. Thou hast willed that through labor and pain I shall walk the upward way; be Thou then my fellow traveler as we go.

Let me face what Thou dost send with strength Thou dost supply;

When Thou prosperest my undertakings, let me give heed, that Thy word may prosper in my heart;

When Thou callest me to go through the dark valley, let me not persuade myself that I know a way round;

Let me not refuse any opportunity of service which may offer itself today . . .

After meditating on this, I left her a message on the opposite blank page: "7:15 A.M. But for this prayer, I would have mailed a letter today to Bishop Joel McDavid withdrawing my name from consideration."

The letter was never mailed. I rested the case. After all, I was born in this Methodist system; the Conference had seen fit to nominate me for bishop; I believed in the system; I believed that God works in and through it; and I would leave it in God's hands.

"Lightning struck," as we say in Methodist circles, on July 18, 1984, at the Southeastern Jurisdictional Conference at Lake Junaluska, North Carolina. My own bishop, Joel McDavid, was in the chair to announce the sixth ballot. I had been elected a bishop in the United Methodist Church.

The die was cast. The affirmation of my colleagues in itself was reassuring, and I had the feeling deep inside that this must be what God wanted me to do. Of one thing I was sure: Whatever this event led to, God would be there for me. I went forth in the confidence of the Ephesian benediction: "Now to him who by the power at work within us is able to do abundantly far more than all that we ask or imagine . . ." (3:20)

Significantly, it was the bicentennial year of Methodism as a denomination in the United States of America. Bishop William R. Cannon and Bishop Mack Stokes escorted me to the platform, and Bishop Frank Robinson and Bishop Roy Short brought Tuck forward. One of my colleagues said quite aptly as he extended his hand, "The view from here is different."

A couple of days later, six of us were consecrated bishops. I chose our son, Dr. David Jones, and my lifelong friend, the Reverend Wesley Stephens, to stand with me.

A couple of close buddies joked to me afterward, "At the close of the consecration service, we wondered, 'What have we done to Bev?' Then we asked, 'What have we done to the church?' "

I wondered too! A reporter for the newspaper in Winston-Salem, herself about my age, asked me bluntly how old I was. When I said fifty-seven, she retorted, "Not many people your age can get a new job."

Then she probed deeper, "Are you scared?"

I questioned, "How did you know?"

I was overwhelmed by feelings of gratitude and humility. After the balloting was over, we were given our assignments by the Committee on Episcopacy, composed of a lay and clergy delegate from each of the seventeen conferences. I was assigned to the Western North Carolina Conference, with offices in Charlotte and Lake Junaluska to boot. That beautiful place became central in our life and work for the next twelve years. The delegates of Western North Carolina welcomed us warmly at a reception and assured us of their hospitality and support, which proved to be unfailing.

Riding Loose in the Saddle

Will Adler tells of an occasion when British Prime Minister Winston Churchill was looking out the window of his office with a friend. Sir Stafford Cripps, pompous chancellor of the exchequer, was striding majestically along Picadilly Circus with his derby hat at a jaunty angle. Churchill observed: "There, but for the grace of God, goes God."

The danger is universal. Just the other day a colleague said of a mutual friend who was wrapped up in feelings of self-importance, "He believes everything he thinks of himself."

Many years ago I heard the late Ernest Rogers, beloved journalist in Atlanta, make a speech on the subject, "Humor Is No Laughing Matter." It is one of life's saving graces. God gave us a sense of humor to keep us from going mad, and driving others the same way. The Reverend Dr. Harold Bales, a colleague of mine in the Western North Carolina Conference, has made it his avowed purpose to eradicate the "heresy of humorless religion." I have found, especially as I grow older, that life is more difficult to the degree I take myself too seriously.

During my last worship service at Northside United Methodist Church before taking on the temporal and spiritual leadership of the Western North Carolina Conference, Dr. Tom Whiting, my district superintendent and intimate friend, knowing my compulsive nature, offered a prayer imploring our Lord on my behalf, "In the vernacular of the Old West, help him to ride loose in the saddle."

Over and over God has prodded me at that point. Many experiences have kept me loose and lighthearted. I never will forget Mrs. Lillian Carter's response to my introduction of her at a banquet at Decatur First United Methodist Church when I was pastor there. Her son, Jimmy, was governor of Georgia, and she had just returned, at age sixty-eight, from two years of service in the Peace Corps in India. She had broken a foot while there and was walking with a crutch.

I gave her a fulsome introduction and helped her as she hobbled to the mike. She paused ceremonially, then turned to me with a devilish grin and exclaimed, "Where did you get all that crap?" The crowd roared! She had 'em with her from then on, for sure.

As bishops we engage in countless ceremonies, consecrating everything from cathedrals to cribs. Soon after I arrived on the scene in North Carolina, the sanctuary of Saint Paul United Methodist Church in Newton burned. It was a small congregation, and the people themselves rebuilt it. The district superintendent and I drove up to reconsecrate it. We were due there at 3 P.M., and were running late. It was mid-July, and the people waited outside in 100-degree heat for me to come and cut the ribbon across the front door.

A teenage boy stood at the entrance to the already jammed parking lot in back of the sanctuary. He pointed to the only empty spot along a fence about seventy-five yards away where he wanted me to park. I said to the district superintendent, "We don't have time to go down there. I'm just going to make a place right here."

I began to maneuver the car, and the young fellow came running toward us. The district superintendent jumped out from the passenger seat and exclaimed, "Son, this is the bishop."

The boy came up to my door, and I rolled down my window and greeted him heartily.

"Are you the bishop?" he asked.

"You betcha, son," I responded.

"Well, I'm glad to meet you, but you still got to park down yonder by that fence."

And I did! That dutiful parking attendant wasn't the last person to tell me where to go in my years as an active bishop!

Humor is a lubricant that makes life run more smoothly. I've seen it work beautifully in meetings that got very tense.

You can hardly imagine the stress that builds up when a bishop and a bunch of district superintendents have to make 200 pastoral changes. Once we were all but cursing each other when one district superintendent brought blessed relief by blurting out, "What some of these churches need is not new preachers but new congregations!" Another time the cabinet was trying its best to place a chronically ineffective minister, who had bounced from church to church like a ball in a pinball machine. When pushed to the wall to explain the minister's ineptness, the district superintendent said, "He does the best he can. He just operates out of a mighty small can."

It's been said that laughter is God's hand on the shoulder of a troubled world. We don't grow old and stop laughing. We stop laughing and grow old. Those who laugh . . . last.

You Bet Your Life

As we drove up Interstate 85 from Atlanta to Charlotte, the last day of August, along the side of the highway I spotted a billboard that read: THERE IS NO HEAVIER BURDEN THAN A GREAT OPPORTUNITY.

Ten miles later the same words appeared on another sign. Several more times before we arrived in Charlotte we saw the same sign, as if the message was meant especially for Tuck and me.

Shortly before this book went to press, I was talking about it with Dr. Fred Davison, former president of the University of Georgia and now president and CEO of the National Science Center foundation. I told him how I arrived at the book's title, and he shared with me his motto: "No risk, no progress." He said he once quoted that to Dr. Edward Teller, known as the father of the hydrogen bomb. Dr. Teller replied, "No! No! Not 'no risk, no progress.' 'No risk, no life.' "

Faith is self-authenticating. When God called Moses to lead his people out of bondage in Egypt, Moses asked Him, "Who shall I tell them sent me?"

God said to him, "I AM WHO I AM" (Exodus 3:14).

Scholars tell us that really means, "Moses, no matter where you go or what may happen, I will be there for you."

Later on, when Moses died on Mount Nebo, short of the Promised Land, God said to Joshua, whom He chose to take Moses' place, "Be strong and courageous; do not be frightened or dismayed; for the Lord your God is with you wherever you go" (Joshua 1:9).

As I have ventured forth, I have found that God's promises become facts. He gives us strength day by day, and whatever He commands, He provides the power to do. Paul called it "the equipping of the saints." We do not really experience the power of God until we attempt that which is greater than we can do in our own strength. As the TV ad says, "The greatest risk is to take none."

In his second letter to his young son in the gospel, Timothy, the Apostle Paul reminds him of his heritage, his gift, and his ordination. Then he goes on to say, "For God did not give us a spirit of cowardice, but rather a spirit of power and of love and of self-discipline" (1:7). Furthermore, he admonishes

Timothy to take his share of suffering, "Relying on the power of God, who saved us and called us with a holy calling, not according to our works, but according to his own purpose and grace" (1:8-9).

There is a beautiful allusion to what I came to experience and to which I can testify, in the book of Hebrews, the eleventh chapter. The writer calls the roll of stalwarts of the faith through the centuries. He speaks of Gideon, Samson, David, and others "who through faith conquered kingdoms, administered justice, obtained promises, shut the mouths of lions, quenched raging fire, escaped the edge of the sword, won strength out of weakness . . ." (11:33, 34). I have not shut the mouths of lions or quenched raging fire or escaped the edge of a sword, but I have won strength out of weakness.

The story of Mary McCleod Bethune never ceases to inspire me. This gallant woman grew up amid the cotton fields of a South Carolina plantation in the 1870s, the last of seventeen children, and the first in her family to be born out of slavery. The church saw great promise in her and provided for her higher education, after which she founded what is now Bethune Cookman College in Daytona Beach, Florida. She became adviser to three presidents of the United States, and was the first person of color to have a statue erected on public ground in her honor in Washington, D.C. To her vast legacy she added this benediction: "Walk bravely in the light. Faith ought not be a puny thing. If you believe, believe like a giant. And may God grant you—not peace—but glory!"

What Do Bishops Do?

United Methodists from across the world filled Public Hall in Cleveland, Ohio, for the quadrennial General Conference in May 2000. For me, memories of a half century earlier came flooding back. I went around to the back of the horseshoe-shaped arena—as far from the speaker as you could get—and found the section where I had sat with a delegation of nearly 100 youths from north Georgia in 1947 for the greatest youth conference I ever attended. Ten thousand young Methodists from all over the nation had traveled to Cleveland for the week between Christmas and New Year's.

The high point for many of us was a sermon by Bishop Richard Raines. He challenged us to make a difference—to be salt and light and leaven in society. He gave us an illustration that I never forgot.

"Your cross," he said as he dramatically crossed his two forefingers, "is where your ability and the world's need intersect."

For half a century I have built my ministry on that reality, ever focusing on the intersection of the world's need and my ability.

There is a saying that bishops either grow or swell. I adopted the style of one of my heroes, the Reverend Gerald Kennedy, who described himself as a "non-bishopy bishop." When I was consecrated a bishop in 1984, I resolved always to grow, while seeking opportunities to match my strengths with the needs of the Conference and the world at large.

Quite frankly, I wasn't exactly sure what to expect or what would be expected of me. One of my colleagues was in conversation with a group of boys and girls, and she asked them, "What do bishops do?"

After some silence, a precocious kid spoke up and said, "They move diagonally." At times that does help!

While I understood more about the job than that young fellow who obviously was acquainted with chess, I had much to learn, and I knew it. The word in the New Testament for bishop is *episcopas*, Greek for "overseer." The bishop is the chief shepherd, or general superintendent, of the churches and institutions of the denomination in a geographical region called a conference. In my case, the Western North Carolina

Conference consisted of forty-four counties from Greensboro to the Tennessee border. It was headquartered in Charlotte, and had 280,000 members and 1,150 churches. I followed in the train of an illustrious succession of episcopal leaders, including Bishop L. Scott Allen, Bishop Earl G. Hunt, and the late Bishop Nolan B. Harmon, who died at age 101. I officiated at his burial in Roanoke, Virginia, in 1996. He used to say, "If the Western North Carolina Conference isn't the best conference in Methodism, it is second to none." What a joy it was to spend my entire active episcopate, twelve years, in that beautiful "land of the sky." The norm is eight years, but I was privileged to stay for an additional quadrennium because of a special initiative we were pursuing in evangelism and church growth.

When I walked up the steps to the Conference office to begin my tenure on the last day of August 1984, Bishop Allen, my immediate predecessor, was there to greet me. This noted African-American from Georgia was retiring after many years of courageous and distinguished leadership in the Methodist Church. Bishop Allen is not a demonstrably emotional person, but a tear welled up in his eye as he spoke.

"Bev, this is a great conference, and I've had eight wonderful years here. My one disappointment has been our inability to get anything significant going in the area of evangelism and church growth. I hope you will major in that."

Church leaders, both lay and clergy, came to me during the first month reiterating Bishop Allen's call to make evangelism and church growth our top priority.

I felt like a baseball batter with a pitch thrown right into his "wheelhouse." My emphasis as a pastor for thirty-five years had been church growth, not just numerically, but spiritually, programmatically, and missionally.

During the first four years we did a lot of research, inventory, and visioning. We were determined to make it holistic and inclusive, not just chalking up statistics. We knew we had to go deeper to go further. Our approach was theological and spiritual, bathed in prayer.

The General Board of Discipleship was about to project a denomination-wide program of congregational development. They asked if they could work in tandem with us as a pilot project. We made one of our clergy, the gifted Dr. Don Haynes, director of congregational development, and organized a strong, representative council of lay and clergy leaders to map out strategy, execute a plan of action, raise and allocate funds, and supervise initial construction.

Together Dr. Haynes and I led rallies in all fourteen districts. We involved young and old in an all-inclusive effort called Vision 2000.

The crusade revitalized the Conference. Membership increased, reversing a slow but steady decline and resulting in a net gain of more than 8,000 and thirty new congregations: twenty brand-new, and ten either relocated, merged, or both. Over half of the more than seventy United Methodist conferences in the United States adopted the program.

Upon my retirement I was deeply gratified when the Conference established the L. Bevel Jones Endowment for Congregational Development with an initial investment of $200,000. The total is now approximately $1 million.

The bishop is charged with the temporal and spiritual leadership of the connection. The aim is to be a servant leader, an instrument of God's grace and Holy Spirit among the constituency. We cultivated a sense of ownership and partnership with the laity in the life and work of the larger church. Teaching was pervasive in all we did, and I endeavored to embody the unity that must be ours among ourselves and with God's people everywhere. I preached in a majority of the 1,150 congregations, often two or three churches on a given Sunday, always greeting as many of the people individually as possible.

I conscientiously sought to fulfill the role of "chief pastor" by being a friend of the clergy of the Conference and making myself available for counseling as the needs arose. Of course, the two main responsibilities of the resident bishop of an area are ordaining clergy and appointing them to their respective fields of service. One of the deepest satisfactions of a bishop is getting to know and guide recruits in ministry and receiving them into full membership in the Conference. The service of ordination is by nature the highlight of every Annual Conference session. I shall always cherish the sacred bond established with more than 400 on whom I laid hands, authorizing them to lead the congregations, administer the sacraments, interpret the scriptures, and preach the word.

The key is putting the right persons at the right place at the right time, so far as pastoral appointments are concerned. We averaged moving about 180 pastors each year in June—all at the same time. What a weighty and far-reaching responsibility! It's like putting together the pieces of a jigsaw puzzle. Every appointment is tied in with the others, and the rub is trying to make them all fit together.

The bishop also chooses clergy to serve limited terms as district superintendents—deputies, you might call them. The fourteen district superintendents and I worked collegially guiding the congregations and making the pastoral assignments. We do it, of course, in consultation both with the pastors and with a representative committee in each local congregation. We don't always get it right, and the congregations let us know it. Like a woman who happened to see the bishop before Annual Conference and said, "Bishop, we at Shiloh are aware that you and the cabinet are making appointments for the new year. We're praying for you, and if in your wisdom and the providence of God you send our pastor back, we will say, 'Amen.' But if in your wisdom and the providence of God you transfer our pastor to another church, we will say, 'Hallelujah!' "

In making appointments we earnestly seek God's guidance and discernment, and expect the pastors and congregations to do likewise. A good illustration of the dynamics at work in the appointment process occurred before I became a bishop, when I was on the receiving end of appointments myself. A colleague and I were leaving Annual Conference and discussing his new, rather disappointing appointment, and a third minister walked over and said to my companion, "I don't believe God was in the appointment you were given." To which my friend said, "Well, I'm not sure about that. But one thing I know—God will be in it when I get there."

It is our conviction about the itinerancy that if we, in careful consultation and earnest prayer, make the assignments, and if the pastors accept the appointments prayerfully, and the congregations receive them prayerfully, they become God's will.

The Least of These

The church has afforded me many extraordinary opportunities to learn firsthand about the peoples of earth and to become actively involved in mission. From 1972-1980 I was a member of the United Methodist Committee on Relief, a division of our General Board of Global Ministries. It deals with relief and rehabilitation of victims of natural disasters and with refugee resettlement.

Our leader was the Reverend Dr. J. Harry Haines, a dynamic, indefatigable New Zealander who constantly cautioned us about the danger of compassion fatigue. If we aren't careful, he warned, we get weary of all the suffering around us and become too tired to care. He also coined the term *aiglatson*, which is *nostalgia* spelled backwards. He was forever moving forward! He never let the crises and calamities get him down. Dr. Haines also introduced to me the concept of "thinking globally, acting locally." He knew that God is always bringing order out of chaos, light out of darkness, and good out of evil.

On a visit to Haiti we went to Grace Children's Hospital in Port-au-Prince. A huge ward full of babies in cribs stretched out before us, each one with an active case of tuberculosis, which can be highly contagious. The hospital staff assured us, however, that we need not worry about getting close to the children because they could not cough hard enough to spread the disease. "You are far more likely to contract TB on a city bus or in a crowded store," they said, "than in this hospital. Feel free to touch the babies, and even coddle them."

We walked among the beds in single file, smiling and waving at the kids, some of whom were pulling up to the sides enough to look into our faces. It was a moving experience! When I got to the end of the line, one of my companions, another minister, said, "I noticed you didn't touch any of them. Neither did I."

We both were ashamed. We believed what the hospital attendants had said, and our hearts were stirred by what we saw. Yet we didn't internalize and act on it. We stayed this side of caution.

That craven behavior has haunted me. It is all too typical of many of us who mean well but hesitate to become involved—to get too close to those who are hurting, and thereby risk exposure. Physicians, surgeons, and therapists tell us that the healing process begins by touching the patient at the point of severest pain. How many times we read in the New Testament of Jesus touching persons in need!

Dr. Marian Wright Edelman, president of the Children's Defense Fund, met with a group of us clergy in Charlotte. She called attention to the fact that one out of every five children in the United States lives in poverty. Every thirteen seconds a child is abused, and every seven hours one dies as a result of neglect or mistreatment. Then Dr. Edelman related how she personally marshaled a dozen key leaders in one of our major cities and went with them to visit with children in a crime-infested tenement section. She said these movers and shakers returned moved and shaken. She left us with the challenge to create awareness and arouse action among our congregations, get them out of their comfort zones and into direct contact with the pain and deprivation.

Every one of them is wonderful, proof that God hasn't given up on the human race. But I am concerned, more *for* them than *about* them, especially those described vividly in Ina Hugh's widely heralded *Prayer for Children*, which I quote in part:

> Who are born in places we wouldn't be caught dead; . . .
> Who never get dessert,
> Who watch their parents watch them die, . . .
> Who don't have any rooms to clean up, . . .

Whose nightmares come in the daytime, . . .
Who go to bed hungry and cry themselves to sleep,
Who live and move, but have no being.

She concludes her "poem that will never die" with these words:

We pray for children
who want to be carried,
and for those who must,
For those we never give up on,
and for those who don't get a chance.
For those we smother,
and for those who will grab the hand of anybody
kind enough to offer.

Since Miss Grace Rogers taught us in Vacation Bible School the wonderful song about Jesus loving the little children, all the children of the world, red and yellow, black and white being precious in His sight, I have carried that mental picture with me.

Bishop Kenneth Carder was a prime mover in the current initiative by the Council of Bishops on "Children and Poverty." Bishop Carder says, "My commitment to ministry and economically impoverished persons is built on two foundations—the Bible's witness to Jesus Christ and my own personal experience growing up in poverty." The child of sharecroppers, Carder adds, "Without the church's witness that 'Jesus loves me,' my impoverished world would have defined me. The church accepted me and welcomed my gifts for ministry."

Every child is yours and mine by proxy. And when we care for any of them, we minister to our Lord by proxy. Did He not make that clear when he said, "Inasmuch as you do it to one of the least of these, you do it unto me" (Matthew 25:40).

In Defense of Creation

In 1968, at the height of the Cold War and just five years after the Cuban missile crisis, I was invited to participate in a conference on science for clergy in Oak Ridge, Tennessee. There I met Dr. William G. Pollard, a physicist who worked on the Manhattan Project developing the atomic bomb. Later he was ordained as an Episcopal priest. Dr. Pollard then became president of Oak Ridge Associated Universities at Oak Ridge, Tennessee, pursuing the peaceful uses of nuclear energy.

Two realizations led to his becoming a man of the cloth:

• The intricacy and intelligibility of the universe convinced him of the existence of God.

• The destructive potential of nuclear power caused him

to realize the spirit of God is essential to the maintenance of human life and planet earth.

Seeing Dr. Pollard there for two weeks wearing his clerical collar amidst that thoroughly technological environment confirmed for me the compatibility of authentic science and authentic religion. Notice I said authentic. It is the pseudo intellectual who sees religion and science in conflict.

Nearly two decades later it all came together in an initiative by the Council of Bishops just as I joined that body.

This was 1985, when the nuclear threat hung over us like a Sword of Damocles. President Reagan was advocating huge increases in military spending, including Star Wars technology, and the Soviet Union was responding with its own outrageous armament spending. Our nuclear defense strategy as a nation was predicated for decades upon "mutual assured destruction." This posture makes me think of Archie Bunker's solution to the hijacking of airplanes: "Give every passenger a gun." We had so many nuclear warheads deployed in silos, on submarines around the globe, and on bombers, that if the Soviets attacked, we could virtually obliterate their nation. The Soviets, likewise, could wreak havoc on the United States and Western Europe if we dared attempt a "first strike."

We Methodist bishops, after intensive study and astute counsel, believed this practice to be seriously flawed. In a four-page pastoral letter titled "In Defense of Creation: the Nuclear Crisis and a Just Peace," we concluded that nuclear deterrence had become "a dogmatic license for perpetual hostility between the superpowers and for their rigid resistance to significant measures of disarmament."

Further, in a 100-page foundation document, we stated, "the Creation itself is under attack. Air and water, trees and fruits and flowers, birds and fish and cattle, all children and youth, women and men live under the darkening shadows of a threatening nuclear winter."

We also addressed the inequities created because of the arms race. "Justice is forsaken in the squandering of wealth in the arms race while a holocaust of hunger, malnutrition, disease, and violent death is destroying the world's poorest people."

Our stance against deterrence was considered radical by many. Even the Roman Catholic bishops, who had previously denounced the nuclear buildup, did not go that far. I was among a group of our bishops who questioned whether we should discount deterrence as a peacekeeper.

I still had misgivings, but in the end I supported the entire document, a move I expected might cost me the support of some back in North Carolina. It was an opportunity to stand publicly on the side of what I believed to be right, to take a step beyond caution, and accept whatever response might follow.

Let us give thanks that not long after that Mr. Gorbachev's bold initiatives in Glasnost and Peristroika, and our president's and other leaders' positive actions in arms limitations and détente, plus the work of the United Nations paid off. The

Iron Curtain came down, and stockpiles of nuclear armaments on both sides were drastically reduced.

Albert Einstein, who was tempted to back out of the Manhattan Project at Oak Ridge when he began to realize fully the destructive power of the atomic bomb, went on to say, "Everything has changed except our way of thinking. We shall require a substantially new manner of thinking if mankind is to survive."

Years later in presenting the Albert Einstein Peace Award to Joseph Cardinal Bernadine of Chicago (formerly vice president of the Christian Council of Metropolitan Atlanta), Norman Cousins said it may well be that Cardinal Bernadine represents our best hope for world peace. Certainly the faith community, by nature, is the harbinger of peace with justice. The ancient prophets proclaimed it, and Jesus, the Prince of Peace, personified it.

More important than being a hawk or a dove is being an owl. The code of the Peace Corps is good regimen for us all:

> Learn peace.
> Live peace.
> Labor for peace.

The seventh Beatitude (Matthew 5:9) is the moral mandate of our time: "Blessed are the peacemakers . . ."

Wanted—Leadership

Sports are woven into the fabric of my being. I love any form of athletic competition, exulting in the exploits of the champion and pulling for the underdog. My first love is baseball. I had the high privilege of offering the prayer at the first official game inaugurating Major League baseball in Atlanta. The Braves opened the 1966 National League season against the Pittsburg Pirates, dedicating the new Atlanta-Fulton County Stadium, the night of April 2, 1966. For over a decade, Dean David Collins of Saint Philips Cathedral and I served as chaplains of the Braves 400 Booster Club. We got to know the Braves personnel and became close friends with Milo Hamilton, "Voice of the Braves," and his associate, Ernie Johnson. I was pastor to Milo's family, and he was master of ceremonies at three great all-sports banquets at Decatur First United Methodist Church. Milo was inducted into the Baseball Radio Hall of Fame in 1992, after becoming the Voice of the Houston Astros, a position he still holds.

In the early 1970s another great friend came back to Atlanta, Clyde King, former pitcher for the Brooklyn Dodgers. I had gotten to know Clyde when he managed the Atlanta Crackers in the 1950s and together with Norman Vincent Peale launched him on a speaking tour that continued in a stellar career climaxing as the general manager of the New York Yankees. Clyde is a devout Christian, and he has a book titled *A King's Life*.

During the early 1970s the Braves 400 Club sponsored Old Timers' Games. The Braves' management turned the clubhouse over to us, and we had a wonderful time visiting with the stars of the '40s, '50s, and '60s. One year Joe Dimaggio was the featured celebrity, and I was accorded the privilege of escorting him to the field after all the others had gone ahead.

The "Yankee Clipper" was always the last to be presented, so he and I stayed in the dressing room until just a few minutes before he was to make his appearance. I had failed to check the underground layout of the stadium carefully and was befuddled when we walked out and saw several unmarked tunnels along the main driveway. I led us into what appeared to be the one to the dugout, but I soon saw that we were headed in the wrong direction. I apologized to Dimaggio as we proceeded to another tunnel—fortunately the right one. A man of few words, Joe broke his silence: "Reverend, if you don't know the way to heaven any better than you know the way to the dugout, I'm not sure I would want you as my pastor!"

We found the way and arrived on the minute, making his appearance even more dramatic. That error riveted in my memory how important it is for leaders to be prepared—to know where they are going and how to get there. In what many are calling the postmodern world, there is a heightened hunger for moral discernment and spiritual direction. The masses are yearning for a sense of their own worth, for values that make life worthwhile no matter what, for significant relationships at the deepest level, that make life wholesome for them and their children, for a "balm in Gilead" to heal the hostility that divides families, diminishes neighborhoods, blights cities, and threatens our world.

Our congregations are looking for spiritual leadership in clergy and staff who care, are personal, informed, up-to-date, know what the scriptures say and can relate them to our day. People want guidance in living the life of faith daily and developing inner strength.

Dr. Leander Keck, in *The Church Confident*, a book containing his Lyman Beecher Lectures at Yale Divinity School, says clergy must engender a rediscovery of serious theology in the classical Christian tradition, and at the same time learn how to communicate it effectively, particularly to those outside the church. To do this Dr. Keck adds that we must be persuaded the gospel matters, and that it can make a difference in persons whose lives are in disarray because they lack a personal relationship with God.

This came home to me forcefully in 1994 when I was in Tallin, Estonia with the Executive Committee of the World Methodist Council. The September evening we arrived in that capital city on the southern shore of the Baltic Sea, the *Estonia*, flagship of the fleet of steamships sailing from Tallin to Copenhagen, Stockholm, Helsinki, and other major cities, was in the harbor. Streaming aboard were more than 1,000 passengers. The next morning we awakened to the news that faulty equipment caused that ship to go down in a heavy storm, and 912 people perished. A pall hung over the city like a fog the week we were there.

The afternoon after the tragedy a number of Rotarians in our group attended the local Rotary Club. Seeing this cadre of tourists enter together and learning that they were clergy, the president said, "This is fortunate for us. We don't have a speaker today, and we're not much into religion in this part of the world. One of our members, who is present among us, lost several of his family on that ship last night. We are all grieving over such overwhelming loss. Would one of you mind standing before us and telling us what you believe?"

Dr. John Barrett, seasoned clergyman from the United Kingdom, shared our faith, witnessing to what sustains him in crisis. He testified to our conviction that God has the whole world in His hands, and that nothing can separate us from the love of God that is in Christ Jesus our Lord. Each of us would do well to think about what we might be called on to say in a similar circumstance. As the Apostle Peter urges, "Always be prepared to give an answer to everyone who asks you to give a reason for the hope that you have" (1 Peter 3:15 NIV).

Into the Third Millennium

The people of Shingleroof Campground in Henry County, Georgia, still talk about what happened as I was preaching on a hot August Sunday night in 1990. Camp meeting takes place, as you may know, outdoors under an arbor with sawdust for a carpet. The service started at eight o'clock and included a lot of hymns, special music, introductions, announcements, the offering, and so on. It was 8:45 when I got up to preach. On the first row, about fifteen feet from the pulpit and at the same level, were a dozen kids, and no adults. They were restless at the outset, and by the time I neared the climax of my message, a towhead boy about seven years old ambled through the sawdust up to the pulpit in a kind of daze. I wondered if he was sick or had to go to the bathroom, or was especially moved by my sermon. I did what came naturally. I stopped preaching, stepped over to the chancel rail, and said, "Young man, what can I do for you?" Just as innocently and earnestly as you please, he looked at me and asked plaintively, "IS IT ABOUT OVER?"

Well, it was then, for sure! And so is our journey through these pages together.

Returning to Atlanta after my active episcopate in North Carolina was like a martin returning to its gourd. I still have the title "bishop," but as a colleague says, it is like having the reins in your hands but no horses in harness. Someone else observed that in retirement you go from being a peacock to a feather duster.

I became bishop in residence at Decatur First United Methodist Church, and also bishop in residence at the Candler School of Theology. At the convocation beginning the 1996-97 academic year, faculty members were asked to identify themselves. Dr. Brooks Holifield preceded me alphabetically. He stood and announced that he taught history. I then stood, introduced myself, and said, "I *am* history. I graduated from this school forty-seven years ago."

The picture on the front of this book was carefully chosen. I am sitting on the steps of Glenn Memorial United Methodist Church at the main entrance to the Emory Campus— the center of my world. It is from there that I get my orientation to human existence. I have come full circle from student to alumnus to trustee to faculty. I thoroughly relish continuing my education in such a wonderful community of faith, knowledge, inquiry, and service. Emory honors its Methodist heritage and the spiritual and moral principles on which it was established, while exercising responsible but unfettered academic freedom. Dr. James T. Laney, former dean of Candler, president of the university, and U.S. ambassador to South Korea, articulates—indeed, embodies—the ethos of Emory at its best. He calls the "education of the heart," education as a moral endeavor with a sense of citizenship and the common good. Dr. Laney calls attention to the difference between a life style and a life, insisting that a life that opens up "into a larger, more spacious and generous self" is far more important than a gaudy, consumer-oriented life style. His legacy inoculates us against self-aggrandizing "careerism" and inspires in us a sense of vocation.

At the heart of the Christian faith is the conviction that in Christ is the hope of the world. The presence at Candler of Archbishop Desmond Tutu of South Africa for two years heightened that conviction. The public in general, and certainly religious people throughout the world, are aware of the courageous and strategic leadership that he has given the people of his native land, along with Nelson Mandela and others, in bringing about the abolition of apartheid and the new democratic republic of South Africa.

The archbishop has a rare sense of humor, which he exercises as the underside of faith. With sharp satire the Nobel Peace Prize recipient says that when white people came to his country, "We had the land and they had the Bible. They asked us to pray with them. When we opened our eyes, they had the land and we had the Bible." Tutu goes on to say that in the long run they were blessed by that exchange. The truth of scripture brought about their liberation. The archbishop encouraged his colleagues and compatriots in the arduous struggle for freedom not to give up or get discouraged. Said he, "I've read the end of the Book. We win!"

Of course, the end of the Bible is the book of Revelation, which is not an almanac, but a great doxology. It is magnificent imagery inspiring a people persecuted for their faith to remain steadfast against all odds. Their allegiance to Christ is not in vain. As Handel's *Messiah* triumphantly proclaims, "The Lord God Omnipotent reigns!"

This hope lies at the heart of the World Methodist Council, around which much of my ministry has centered for the last twenty-five years. Organized in London in 1881, the Council consists of 500 persons representing 75 member churches (branches of Methodism) in more than 100 nations, comprising 37 million individual members and a constituency of more than 70 million. The council sponsors a world conference every five years. The eighteenth session was held in 2001 in Brighton, England, where more than 3,500 Methodists from 100 nations came to grips with the theme, "Jesus—God's Way of Salvation" through worship, fellowship, study, drama, visioning, and programing. My protege, Dr. Hal Brady, pastor of Saint Luke United Methodist Church in Columbus, Georgia, gave masterful leadership as chairperson of the international program committee. Dr. Frances Alguire, climaxed her tenure as first female chairperson of the Council, and we paid tribute to Dr. Joe Hale, our general secretary since 1976, upon his retirement after a quarter-century of extraordinary leadership. In addition to honoring him with the World Methodist Peace Award, previously presented to former President Jimmy Carter, former Soviet President Mikhail Gorbachev, and other world-renown leaders, we named the headquarters at Lake Junaluska for him and his devoted wife, Mary. Mrs. Hale's faithful service, despite a disabling embolism and stroke in 1996, has been an inspiration to their friends across the world. Tuck and I have enjoyed many memorable experiences with the Hales at their home and abroad.

In 1996, we went to Rio de Janeiro, a megalopolis of more than 10 million persons. If you have ever been there, you know how beautiful it is. Towering over the metro area in the heart of it is Mount Corcavado, and on the summit stands a 100-foot concrete statue of Christ with His arms outstretched. As I stood at the foot of that mammoth monument and looked out at the city below, I remembered the story my friend Andy Kane of Charlotte told of a trip he made to Rio. On a visit to one of the vast slum areas on the back side of Mount Corcavado, conditions were deplorable beyond description—a veritable sea of squalor. The people eked out an existence in hovels not fit for human habitation. Disease was rampant, and death a constant visitor. Despair hung over the area like a heavy fog.

Andy and his friends encountered a community worker and asked how she related to the people living there. She called attention to the wretched conditions and said that the mood was depressive. "Often," she said, "they will point up to the mountain and exclaim, 'Look, even Jesus has turned His back on us!' " For them, so far as their future was concerned, life indeed seemed to be "about over."

But then the community worker smiled and said, "That is not how it is, really. For, you see, Jesus is leading us out of this!"

In the risen Christ, we are endowed with a living hope. Of His Kingdom there shall be no end!

Benediction

As you go, may God go with you.
May God go:
Before you to guide you,
Behind you to guard you,
Beneath you to uphold you,
Above you to inspire you,
Beside you to befriend you, and
Within you to give you peace.

Amen

In 1921, Bev's father, L.B. Jones Jr., stands outside the family's log home in Hickory Flat, Georgia. The car sitting by the front porch later carried him from his charge in northwest Georgia to his new assignment near Augusta.

Bev participated in intramural baseball, track, football, and softball at Emory University, where he was cross-country champion in 1944.

Much of Bev's ministry has been involved with Boy Scouts, Boys Clubs, and YMCA programs.

Bev, his mother, his sister Kathryn, and his father.

Bev and Tuck were married at Decatur First Methodist Church August 12, 1949.

Joe Dimaggio and Bev prior to an Old Timers' Game at Atlanta-Fulton County Stadium.

Arnold Palmer and Bev following the memorial service of Ely Callaway at Callaway Gardens.

God bless you Bev - you are so special to me!

Bill Curry and Bev were close friends through Curry's playing and coaching days at Georgia Tech.

Bev's father was on hand at LaGrange College when Bev received the first of numerous honorary degrees.

A high moment for Tuck and Bev was Bev's election as bishop in 1984.

In 1972, Bev was clergy leader of the Billy Graham Crusade in Atlanta. He and Dr. Graham met with Bishop Arthur J. Moore, a strong supporter of the first Graham Crusade in Atlanta.

When Mother Teresa visited Charlotte, Bev was among the clergy who met with her.

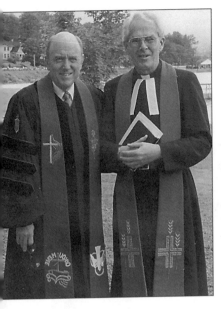

Bishop Peter Storey, of South Africa, instrumental in the dismantling of apartheid, remains an inspiration to Bev.

For two years Bev and Archbishop Desmond Tutu were colleagues at Emory University.

Bishop Rueben P. Job welcomes Bev as president of United Methodist Communications.

For twelve years Bishop L. Bevel Jones III addressed the Western North Carolina Conference of the United Methodist Church at Lake Junaluska, North Carolina.

With son David's appointment to an Atlanta area United Methodist Church, Bev and Tuck now have all of their children and grandchildren close by.